D1276361

Ancient Peoples and Places

THE GREEKS

IN THE WEST

General Editor

DR. GLYN DANIEL

Ancient Peoples and Places

THE GREEKS

IN THE WEST

A. G. Woodhead

81 PLATES
20 LINE DRAWINGS
6 MAPS
AND A TABLE

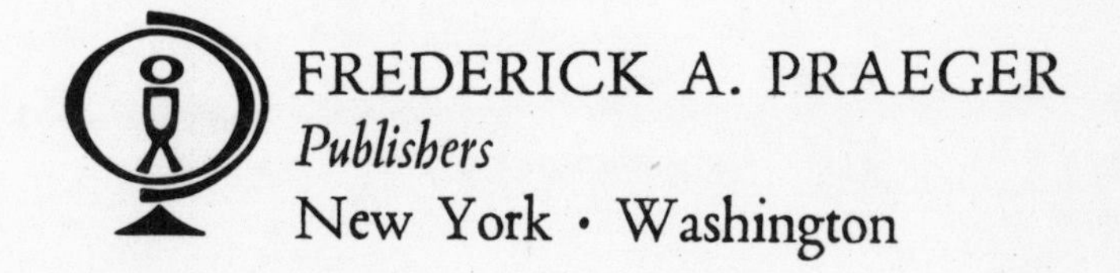

THIS IS VOLUME TWENTY-EIGHT IN THE SERIES
Ancient Peoples and Places
GENERAL EDITOR: DR. GLYN DANIEL

BOOKS THAT MATTER
Published in the United States of America
in 1962 by Frederick A. Praeger, Inc. Publishers
111 Fourth Avenue, New York, N.Y. 10003
Second printing, 1966

Library of Congress Catalog Card Number: 62-15539

Printed in Great Britain

CONTENTS

ILLUSTRATIONS

FIGURES

For Dora

Preface

THIS BOOK has been written with three principal objects in mind. First, it aims to provide for the ever-increasing number of 'travellers in antique lands' a survey which, for those interested in the Greek remains of the western Mediterranean, will offer a fuller yet convenient background to what they find on the ancient sites. Its second aim is to provide the classical student with a short conspectus of the history and attainments of the western Greeks which may serve as a basis for closer study of particular details: and last, though by no means least, it seeks to break new ground in isolating the distinctive features of western Hellas and suggesting some assessment of their relationship to Hellenism as a whole. To attempt this within the limits laid down by the 'Ancient Peoples and Places' series is no doubt rash, and in all probability justice has been done to no single one of the aims outlined. Much has had to be omitted and much treated with an inadequacy it does not deserve. To quote a single example, the fascinating and fruitful excavations conducted during the past few years at Morgantina by successive expeditions sponsored by Princeton University merit more than one or two passing references.

I am, however, grateful to Messrs Thames and Hudson, and to the general editor of the series, Dr Glyn Daniel, for having asked me to write the book. I have enjoyed writing it, and my chief hope is that, with a kindly indulgence towards its numerous shortcomings, its readers will enjoy reading it. I have taken for granted a good many things about Greek life and society in general, in the expectation that those interested will regard this book as something of a complement to R. M. Cook's *The Greeks till Alexander* in the same series, for it would have been pointless to cover similar ground twice.

The list of those who have helped and encouraged me with advice and criticism, or with the provision of information and photographs, is a long one, and a selection of acknowledgements will be found on page 174: but to those whose names appear there, and to others whose assistance has been readily forthcoming on this point or that, I should like to express my lively gratitude. One name, to me the most important, has been reserved for the dedicatory page.

G. W.

A CHRONOLOGICAL TABL

	SICILY	ITALY	THE AEGEAN
			First Olympiad (776)
750		*Ischia founded* (*c.* 750)	
		Cumae founded (750–25)	*Homer and Hesiod*
	Syracuse founded (*c.* 734)	*Taras founded* (706)	*Colonisation of Black Sea area*
700			
	Gela founded (680)		
650			
	Selinus founded (628)		
600		*Massalia founded* (600)	
	Acragas founded (580) *Phalaris*		*Solon archon at Athens* (594)
550			
		Elea founded (*c.* 530)	
	Expedition of Dorieus (510)	*Destruction of Sybaris* (510)	*Democracy at Athens* (*c.* 507)
500			
	Gelon, tyr. of Syracuse (491–78)		*Persian invasions* (490–79)
	Hieron I (478–66)	*Battle of Cumae* (474)	
450	*Ducetius and the Sicel revolt*		
		Thurii founded (444–3)	*Age of Pericles*
	Athenian expedition (415–13)		*Peloponnesian War* (431–04)
400	*Dionysius I* (405–367)	*Samnites and Lucanians subjugate Cumae and other cities*	
	Dionysius II (367–44)	*Syracusan empire in S. Italy*	*Thebes defeats Sparta* (371)
350	*Dion* (358–6)	*Dionysius II at Locri* (356–45)	
	Timoleon (345–*c.* 336)	*Archidamus of Sparta d. in Italy* (338)	*Philip II of Macedon supreme* (338)
300	*Agathocles* (315–289)		*Alexander the Great* (336–23)
	Pyrrhus in Sicily (278–6)	*Pyrrhus aids Taras* (280–75)	*Gallic invasion* (280–78)
	Hieron II, k. of Syracuse (265–15)	*S. Italy Roman territory from* 272	*Rise of Achaean and Aetolian Leagues*
250	*First Romano-Punic war* (264–41)		
	Sicily a Roman province (240)		
	Roman siege of Syracuse (213–11)	*Hannibal in Italy* (218–03)	*Philip V, k. of Macedon* (221–179)
200			*Romans defeat Macedon* (197) *and Syria* (190)
150			*Greece a Roman province* (146)
	Slave revolts (135–2 and 104–1)	*Agrarian unrest* (*Gracchan pd.*)	
100		*S. Gaul a Roman province* (120)	
	Verres propraetor (73–1)	*Civil Wars* (*intermittently*, 80–31)	*Sulla repulses Mithridates* (86–4)
27	*Augustus Caesar founds the Roman Empire*		

EVENTS AND PERSONS

LITERATURE Prose	Poetry	PHILOSOPHY, SCIENCE, ETC.	ART AND ARCHITECTURE	
				750
			Protocorinthian pottery	
				700
				650
			Corinthian pottery	
		Voyage of Colaeus (*c.* 650–30)		
	Arion			600
	Stesichorus		*Temple C at Selinus*	
	Ibycus		*Tem. of Apollo at Syracuse*	550
		Xenophanes	*Red-figure pottery begins*	
	Epicharmus	*Pythagoras*	*Caeretan hydrias*	500
	Pindar		*Olympieum at Acragas*	
	Aeschylus	*Empedocles*	*First theatre at Syracuse*	
	Sophron	*Parmenides*	*Pythagoras (sculptor)*	450
tiochus		*Zeno*	*'Tem. of Neptune' at Paestum*	
		Gorgias	*Finest Syracusan coinage*	400
	Dionysius I		*Dionysius I fortifies Syracuse*	
listus		*Plato in Sicily*	*S. Italian schools of*	
		Archytas	*vase-painting*	350
hanis			*City-rebuilding under Timoleon*	
cus		*Voyage of Pytheas*		300
tander			*Centuripae vases*	
llias			*Theatre-construction in Sicily*	
naeus	*Theocritus*			250
			Hieron II's building programme	
		Archimedes		
				200
		Voyages of Eudoxus		150
				100
			Roman colony at Pompeii	
odorus			*Augustus refounds Tyndaris*	27

CHAPTER I

One World

'They went forth, urged by the love of adventure, by the passion for discovery, by the desire for a freer life in new countries. Wherever they went, they carried with them the traditions, the habits, the ideals of their Mother Country. Wherever they settled they planted a new homeland. And, though mountains and the waste of seas divided them, they never lost that golden thread of the spirit which drew their thoughts back to the land of their birth.'

STANLEY BALDWIN spoke of British colonisation, but his words could as readily refer to the Greeks who left their Aegean cities to found new homes and farm new lands in Sicily and along those coasts of southern Italy later to acquire the name of *Megalê Hellas* or *Magna Graecia.* Surrounded by barbarian strangers, struggling against man and nature for survival, even amid their own mutual enmities and warfare, they never forgot the common bond of their Greekness. Old Greece reacted on them and they on it. They joined in the sacred festivals of the Greek sanctuaries, and welcomed home many a western competitor with crowns of victory from the Greek games. There were times when they stood in need of support from the Greeks of the homeland, and the ties of their common ancestry were always sufficient cause for such appeals for help to be made and answered; and there were times when the Greek new world was summoned to redress the balance of the old.

The distances involved, and the conditions of city-government, made it impossible for a mother-city, even if it so wished, to retain any direct control over a colony. Corinth was unusual in tending to maintain a direct interest in her foundations, and even so made the attempt, without notable success, only with her colonies in the Greek peninsula itself. The over-all pattern was that a settlement, once established, was on its own, without formal ties with its parent. Yet the bonds of sentiment, with a peculiar strength of their own, were able as in modern times successfully to combine unity with diversity, and to ally community of thought and interest with freedom and independence. The framework of Hellas thus remained a single entity, and as Greek civilisation evolved the Greeks of the Tyrrhenian and Ionian seas were no less active in its development than the Greeks of the Aegean. Although in this book the Western Greeks and what they thought and did are considered by themselves, it is the unity of Hellas that is its real theme.

When in 1943 Wendell L. Willkie wrote of the patterns which seemed to be emerging from the trials of war, he gave to his book the title *One World*. Had he not pre-empted it, it might have served as the title of this.

Fig. 1. Sicily

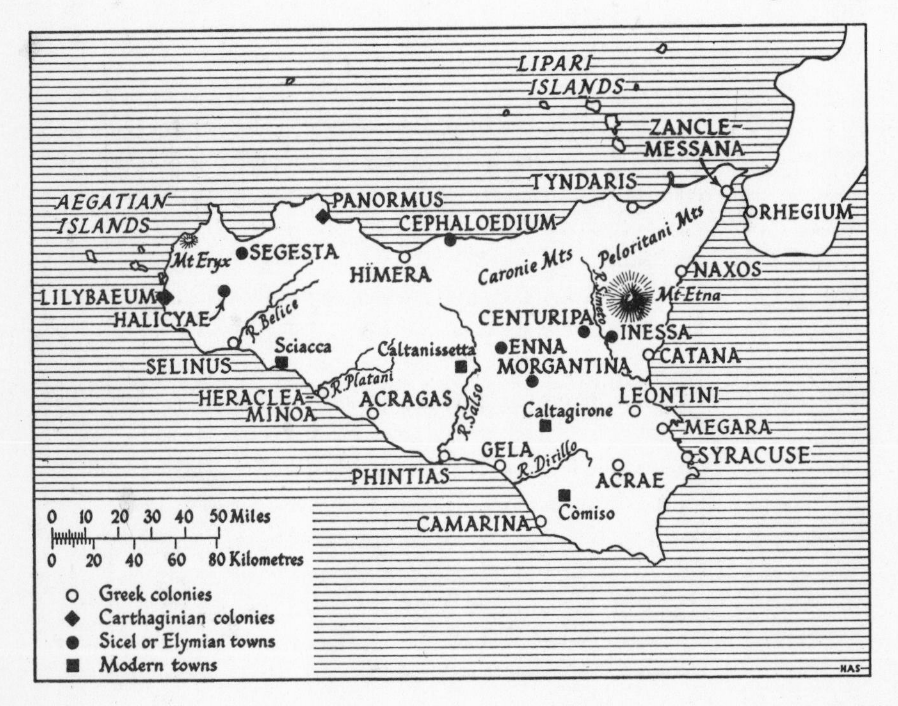

Fig. 2. Magna Graecia

CHAPTER II

Fact and Fiction before the Greek Settlements

FACT

WHEN IN THE COURSE of the eighth century B.C. Greeks from Euboea sailed out to found the first colonies in the western Mediterranean, they were not venturing into the unknown, where no Greek had sailed before. Admittedly it was a bold and venturesome undertaking, to sail westward never to return, intent on founding a new Greek *polis* to reproduce on an alien shore what they had left behind. The new *polis* indeed, as subsequent pages will show, tended to mirror all too faithfully the vices as well as the virtues of the Greek city-state, but the settlers in this case were not, like the Pilgrim Fathers, looking for a land free from persecution, where their settlement might be a new and improved version of its parent. The Greek colonists sought to establish the same pattern of society in a fresh home, looking principally for space in which to live and wider lands for farming and grazing. When they went, they must have drawn upon geographical knowledge already acquired by traders whose ships had by then begun to find their way to profitable harbours in the western sea.

This trade cannot as yet have been extensive. As will be discussed later, it is doubtful whether it should in itself be considered as a motive for the actual settlements, and it is doubtful also how much trade on the sites which were colonised preceded the colonists' arrival. Earlier emphasis on these factors needs modification. But the early voyagers themselves were only following a route already enshrined in Greek tradition, and this tradition probably had its origin in trade conducted in the

Mycenaean period and in the presumed Mycenaean settlement in the west.

Mycenaean penetration of the west seems to have begun in the seventeenth century B.C. A cup found at Monte Sallia near Còmiso has been recognised as an import of the Middle Helladic period, as has a bone sword-pommel from another tomb at the same site, and these provide evidence of contact between Greece and Sicily at least as early as the first part of the sixteenth century. But the majority of the Mycenaean material in the west belongs to the 'Mycenaean period' proper, and in the Lipari islands and islands of Vivara and Ischia off the Italian coast it is fairly equally distributed between Myc. I and II on the one hand, and Myc. III on the other. At other sites the predominant phase is that of Myc. III—more precisely within this limit that of Myc. III*a* (*c.* 1400 B.C.). This is significant, since the great age of Mycenaean trade was that designated Myc. III*b*, and so the western connexions seem to have grown up remarkably early.

Apart from the islands already mentioned, where presumably the Mycenaean traders found safe and advantageous depôts, Mycenaean finds are comparatively restricted in their distribution. A fair amount of pottery has been found in the area of Syracuse (though not in Syracuse itself), with some outlying finds at Agrigento. In Italy a great quantity, to which a Rhodian origin has been ascribed, was discovered at Taranto, and its abundance has led to the supposition that a Mycenaean colony was actually planted there. From this centre it is likely that Mycenaean products reached other sites in Apulia—Leporano, Torre Castelluccia and San Cosimo.

Plate 3

But although the pottery evidence in itself is restricted in amount, much significance has been attached to the supposed influence of Mycenaean or Minoan imports on local products. Reminiscences of Aegean models have been held to have affected the great sword found in the Plemmyrion necropolis south of Syracuse and similar though smaller swords and daggers from elsewhere, and the local pottery of the Middle Bronze Age (the Milazzese culture in the Lipari islands and the Thapsos culture in the area of Syracuse) shows undoubted eastern characteristics. There was some architectural influence also, in forms, style and motifs, especially in the use of the linked spiral decoration well known from Mycenae and in the tholos tombs found at Thapsos and Cozzo del Pantano. The use of this kind of tomb penetrated inland to Caltagirone and impressed itself on a later age, for a series of such tombs at Sant' Angelo Muxaro north of Agrigento belongs to the last stage of pre-Greek Sicily. Of particular interest is the introduction of potters' marks on vases, which is thought to have been adopted from Mycenaean imports. The ubiquitous faience beads, which in a chain of distribution across Europe link Egypt and Britain in continuous evidence of Bronze Age trade, are attested also in the Lipari islands. The British end of this trade connexion is strikingly evidenced by the Mycenaean dagger found at Pelynt in Cornwall, supporting as it does the evidence of the dagger carved on one of the great standing stones of Stonehenge. The Mycenaean material from the Lipari islands is indeed such that a full-scale settlement, as in the case of Taranto, has been suggested for them. A colony has also been proposed for Palermo, though on the more slender basis of two Mycenaean figurines found there.

Plate 4

Plate 1

Plate 2

It may be worth adding that while the principal western relationships are with the Mycenaean culture, there are also traces of contact with Minoan Crete, and these also have left their mark on tradition. But in the past, perhaps under the influence of the tradition, they have been overestimated, and effectively they amount to little more than a handful of Late Minoan I sherds from Lipari. From this meagre evidence there can be no argument as to direct trade with Crete, and other alleged examples of Cretan influence have been better explained on a Mycenaean basis.

The extent to which actual colonisation, rather than trade of particular intensity, ought to be postulated remains an open question. Scholars have perhaps been over-eager to recognise colonies where at most small trading-depôts should be envisaged. The Mycenaean imports and influences group themselves in the main into fairly clearly defined areas, where trade between the Aegean world and particularly advanced or receptive natives had been worked up. At Taranto, the most likely candidate as a regular Mycenaean colony, the picture has been further blurred by a remarkable stratification of finds from excavations conducted at the beginning of the century which associated Mycenaean and Protocorinthian sherds in the same stratum. This led T. J. Dunbabin to suggest that 'contact with the Aegean was not broken for long, if at all, between the Mycenaean imports of the late thirteenth century and the coming of the Greeks': but the pottery evidence may well have been confused at the time of discovery. The pattern here as elsewhere seems to be that on the collapse of Mycenaean power in Greece contacts were broken. Traces of Aegean influence remained in some architectural and ceramic usages and styles, but it was not until the late Geometric period in Greece that pottery of Greek manufacture began to find its way once more to the west.

Meanwhile, for the Greeks the west bequeathed its memories and became a land of wonder and romance. The appeal of its legendary attractions was undoubtedly one of the various factors which drew them to settle there in the 'colonising period', for by then it was already enshrined in some of their principal folk-stories, and later ages extended and transformed much of that store of legend to suit differing purposes of their generation, adapting particular stories in such a way as to enhance a local tradition, explain a local custom, or lay claim to an ancient and noble origin for family or city. It thus becomes a matter of some difficulty to disentangle the various versions at their various stages and to discover what historical basis, if any, may be attributed to them.

FICTION

By the time that Virgil described Rome's Trojan origin and linked its foundation with that of the hereditary enemy, Carthage, by means of Aeneas' wanderings and renunciation of Dido, the saga of the west had come through a long development. In its earliest and, to this day, its most magical form it lives in Books IX–XII of the *Odyssey,* in which Odysseus tells King Alcinous and the court in Phaeacia of the adventures which had befallen him since he and his comrades had sailed homewards from Troy. That the *Odyssey* is formed out of many strands of folk-poetry is generally agreed. Some of its elements undoubtedly belong not to the Western Mediterranean but to the Black Sea, and indeed the origin of it all has been so ascribed. But parts of it must surely have always been rooted in memories of the west, and the whole series of adventures came, in the end, to be located there—even the enchantress Circe, whose brother Aeetes was king of Colchis in the Caucasus and father of Medea, came to have her magic castle at Circeii on the Campanian coast, not far from where, at Cumae, Odysseus was able to enter the world of the dead. The impressive beauty or perilous grandeur of so much of the Italian and Sicilian land- and sea-scape makes it easy for the imagination to accept the identifications which have been proposed for Odysseus' ports of call. Scylla and Charybdis are inescapably to be associated with the straits of Messina and the Cyclopes with Mt Etna, below which the Isole Ciclopi off Acitrezza recall the fury of the blinded Polyphemus in his vain attempt at revenge. Other identifications may be more speculative though no less attractive. Off Positano, Li Galli are the perfect rocks for the Sirens' song. Calypso's island, Ogygia, perhaps as far away as

ODYSSEUS

Fig. 3

Fig. 3. Odysseus and the Sirens, from the stamnos by the Siren Painter, early fifth century B.C. Found at Vulci, and now in the British Museum. Height of vase, 35.2 cm.

Gibraltar or Tenerife, has also been thought of as somewhere off Cutrò, on the southern coast of Calabria, while the land of the Lotus-eaters, plausibly to be identified with Jerba island, off the south-east coast of Tunisia, suggests that Mycenaean sailors were not unacquainted with the shore of Africa. It is of course significant that Odysseus' home was in Ithaca, remote to the ordinary Greek, from which the voyage to the west was not difficult; and it is even more interesting, perhaps, that the islands of Aeolus, the home of the winds that would speed a trader or traveller on his way, are the very places to which, on the evidence, Mycenaean trade came—and through which Mycenaean goods may well have passed on their route to northern Europe.

Homer clearly lacked precise knowledge of the west. Odysseus' father is said to have had a Sicilian woman-servant, and 'Sicania' is once mentioned, but both references occur in the last book of the epic, in which they seem to be intrusive elements, anachronisms in the picture given by the work as a whole. The rationalising influence of later writers, especially those interested in co-ordinating the legends and correcting their geography and chronology, has produced a number of variant versions. Thus the land of the Laestrygonians, which Bérard locates in northern Sardinia by the straits of Bonifacio, was placed in Sicily by Thucydides, more precisely around Leontini by Theopompus, and at Formiae in Campania by the Latin authors, among them Cicero and Horace. A late addition to the epic cycle, written in the sixth century B.C. by Eugammon of Cyrene under the title *Telegoneia,* told the story of Telegonus, the son of Odysseus and Circe. Subsequent embroidery gave him brothers like Auson, Latinus and Rhomus, from whom the Ausonii, the Latins and the Romans themselves could be derived: but it is fair to add that Latinus may make his appearance as early as Hesiod and form one of the more ancient elements in the legend.

THE ARGONAUTS

If parts of the story of Odysseus underwent, at a stage almost farther back than we can see, some transference of locale from the Black Sea to the shores of Italy and its islands, it is possible in the legend of the Argonauts to see the very same phenomenon, but at a much later and more sophisticated period. The whole saga of Jason, Medea and the Golden Fleece is concerned with the shores of the Caucasus and the dangers of the journey through the Dardanelles and Bosporus to a land of wealth and opportunity beyond. These adventures were thought to belong to the first or second generation before Odysseus, for Heracles was an Argonaut and he is variously assigned to the one or the other. By the time of Apollonius Rhodius and his *Argonautica* (mid third century B.C.) the legend was extended by a story that the Argo returned up the Danube, *sailing* through to the Adriatic and so home. Apollonius, who would have met this tradition already in Theopompus, added to it by sending the Argonauts along the river Po and down the Rhône. Timaeus the Sicilian historian improved even on this far-reaching system by describing their voyage as up the river Don, with a portage at its upper limit to another river which brought them to the streams of Ocean—from which point it was a straightforward journey round to Gibraltar and into the Mediterranean. To carry conviction with the reader who might demand scientific history he notes the veneration of the Celts for the Dioscuri and includes epigraphical evidence in the shape of an inscribed bronze tripod at Euesperides (*Benghazi*) in Cyrenaica, unfortunately, as he adds, not still extant. The legend of the Argonauts in the west is thus the literary creation of a later age, of no value for the early memories of the western seas.

ARETHUSA

With some of the stories from these sources it is difficult to judge how far back they go and in what form. The legend of the nymph Arethusa, the goddess of Syracuse so beautifully portrayed on the finest Syracusan coinage, is a case in point. Her story was that, being a nymph who lived near Olympia in the Peloponnese, she attracted the admiration of the river-god Alpheus. Fleeing to elude his unwanted attentions she plunged into the sea, emerging at Syracuse where she was transformed into a spring of fresh water which rises beside the shore on the island of Ortygia. Alpheus, who kept up his pursuit, emerged offshore not far away. This legend goes back at least to the sixth century B.C. Pausanias quotes an oracle in connexion with the foundation of Syracuse by Archias, and if this has any basis in fact it would make the Arethusa story antedate 734 B.C. Timaeus sought evidential support for this too, by saying that when sacrifices are made in Olympia the waters of the Syracusan spring become cloudy in common with those of the Alpheus, and that a golden bowl which fell into the Alpheus reappeared

Plate 80

Plate 81

later in the fountain. For this both Polybius and Strabo took him vigorously and justly to task. It may, however, be no accident that some of the strongest Mycenaean contacts were with the Sicilians of the Thapsos culture in the Syracusan area. Bowls from the Peloponnese might indeed, though by more prosaic methods, have reappeared beside the waters of Arethusa.

HERACLES

Of the legends of Heracles it is hard to speak with any coherence or clarity. That of the garden of the Hesperides is a recognisable 'triumph-over-death' folk-tale, and an understandable part of folklore also is a cosmography which upholds the firmament on the shoulders of a giant. Their locale could be placed in a mysterious west without any inference of half-forgotten memories of the Atlas mountains or an enterprising Mycenaean voyage beyond the 'Pillars of Hercules' to the Canary Islands (if the Fortunate islands of the dead and the land of the Hesperides may be equated with these). Such geographical co-ordination more properly belongs to a later stage in the tradition. In any case, while many of the Heracles-tales are concerned with the Greek peninsula itself or with the Black Sea area, legend connected the hero with the far west no less than with the far east, and Heracles clearly suffered or profited from a great accretion of diverse material. But there can be no doubt that the western aspect of the legend was an early introduction which might well have preceded the classical Greek colonisation of the west. For example, Stesichorus sets Erytheia (from which Heracles drove the cattle of Geryon) not far from Tartessus, and this could represent a well-established picture now acquiring precision of detail; for Hesiod makes Geryon the son of the Ocean nymph Callirrhoe and places 'sea-girt' Erytheia beyond the streams of Ocean. In the course of his journey Heracles visited Italy, and the developed saga connects him with Rome, where he rid the place of the brigand Cacus and founded a colony, with Latium, with Campania (where Herculaneum was another of his foundations), with Croton,

Syracuse and elsewhere. Many local hero-stories were undoubtedly systematised in this way, and there is no clue to be had from them concerning the Greeks' early acquaintance with this area.

TROJAN AND GREEK HEROES

The Aeneas legend, at any rate in the form familiar in the *Aeneid,* is also hardly in point here. The introduction of Dido to it seems not to antedate Timaeus, who found himself in difficulties over the reconciliation of the dates of the Trojan War with those of the foundations of Rome and Carthage. But the notion of a Trojan migration to the west goes back a long way. For Thucydides the Elymians in Sicily were Trojans who had fled westwards, and the cult of Aphrodite on Mt Eryx (*Erice*) was held to have a Trojan origin. Aeneas' connexion with Latium is also known as early as the fifth century B.C. Legends of city-foundations carried out by heroes from the Trojan War are persistent in the west. Quite apart from Aeneas and the Trojans, there were Greeks who found themselves in western waters. Metapontum is said to have been settled by companions of Nestor, the aged king of Pylos, and in this case a version of the story goes back to the Syracusan Antiochus. Epeius and Philoctetes also came to Italy, the one founding a city named Lagaria near Metapontum and the other colonising the Croton district. But these and similar tales have no foundation when related to the archaeological evidence of the sites themselves, and though valiant efforts have been made to sift some grains of historical truth from the legendary chaff it can hardly be claimed that the results have justified the trouble.

Plate 36

THE RHODIANS

Only in two remaining instances is it possible to suggest that something—some misty remembrance of a once-historical event —might underlie the existing story. One concerns the persistent connexion of the Rhodians with western settlement. Archaeologically they have been connected with the Mycenaean material at Taras, and Denys L. Page has recently emphasised the importance of their place in the Mycenaean world. Apart from their colonisation of Gela in the historical period they are linked with the coasts of Spain and Gaul before the Phocaean settlements there. But they are said to have sailed under Tlepolemus, their leader in the Trojan War, to settle the Spanish islands (*Balearics*), Parthenope (*Naples*), Elpia in Apulia, Siris (also connected with Calchas and the Trojans) and Sybaris, and they fight beside Philoctetes near Croton. It is not perhaps too much to credit that below the embroidered and systematised versions collected by later writers such as Strabo in the Augustan period, who have preserved the varying traditions for us, a trace of genuine antiquity may yet remain.

THE CRETANS

Most tantalising of all is the tradition, of which Herodotus gives the first literary version, which links Crete and Sicily —the flight of Daedalus to the west, where he was received by Kokalos king of the Sicans at his city of Inykon. Daedalus built for Kokalos the impregnable fortress of Kamikos, and when Minos the Cretan king arrived (at Heraclea Minoa) in pursuit of Daedalus, Kokalos enticed him to Kamikos and murdered him there, sending his body back to the Cretan forces with an explanation of death by misadventure. A temple to Aphrodite which the Cretans built in honour of their dead king was held in great respect by the Sicans, and survived until it was destroyed by Theron, tyrant of Acragas. The archaeological evidence is Mycenaean, not Minoan; but it has been suggested that Sant' Angelo Muxaro may be Kamikos, and the tradition of Mycenaean craftsmanship, as is known from the late tholos tombs, died hard. Although it is correct to follow Dunbabin in being sceptical of any alleged visits of Greeks to Italy in the prehistoric period where literary sources alone provide the evidence, there is in this case just sufficient in the available archaeological material for one to fancy that, through the mists of romance and myth, something real and tangible is there to be grasped.

CHAPTER III

Colonisation and Settlement

COLONISATION AND THE GREEKS

IN HIS RÉSUMÉ of the early development of Greece, Thucydides remarks, 'It was with difficulty that Greece settled down, and it took a long time, once the migrations were over; but then the Greeks sent out colonies. The Athenians settled Ionia and most of the islands, while Italy and Sicily were settled for the most part by the Peloponnesians—who also made some settlements in Greece itself. All these foundations took place later than the Trojan War.' The 'age of colonisation', as modern research has confirmed, belongs to the period when the Hellenes were already settled in Hellas on a pattern resembling the political 'map' of the classical period and when, by virtue of that settlement and the resulting increase in population, they were beginning to find that country too small. Colonisation and movement of population were always features of Hellenic life, and Thucydides has combined in his statement two phases of a process which extended over a long period, for it was from the eighth to the sixth century that the great expansion outside the Aegean area took place.

LAND SHORTAGE

Agriculturally, Greece is a comparatively poor country. In a few generations of settled existence the pressure of an expanding population on its resources could become uncomfortable, and while war, disease, a high rate of mortality among infants and women in childbirth, and other constant factors would play their part in checking the rate of growth, it is not surprising that a demand for more land should have made itself felt. Subdivision of family plots among many sons reduced the third or fourth generation to a dangerously low level of subsistence, and Hesiod emphasises the desirability of having no more than a single heir. Tenure or acquisition of land through inheritance or citizenship-grant was the most closely guarded of all private rights, and boundary disputes were a major cause of inter-city warfare. Where agricultural land was most scarce the difficulties were felt at an early stage. Neither Thessaly nor Boeotia, for instance, joined in this colonising movement; but the isthmus cities of Corinth and Megara, the Achaeans on their narrow strip beside the Corinthian Gulf, and the Chalcidians and Eretrians from mountainous Euboea, were all prominent in it.

ADVENTURE AND ENTERPRISE

The general settlement of Greece not only made the movement of population more necessary; it also made it more practicable. It was now safer to navigate the seas, and easier to engage in international relationships. The beginnings of exploration and trade brought travellers into contact with likely areas for settlement, and a general spirit of adventure added further impetus. This was the dawn of classical Hellas, and the day was yet fresh and young. There was a youthful readiness to venture out which is recaptured but rarely, as by the Portuguese navigators of the fifteenth century or the American pioneers of the nineteenth.

This personal element, indeed, probably deserves more stress than it has received. It is fashionable to look for great impersonal causes and trends which, singly or in combination, produce a human response, and the economic considerations already discussed fall into that category. But in fact many of the colonies, as will appear, had their origins in purely individual enterprise or extraordinary happenings. The Phocaeans moved *en masse* to Corsica because they would not endure Persian domination; Taras was founded because of doubts regarding the legitimacy of some of the young Spartans. In 480 B.C. Themistocles could threaten that the entire Athenian population would sail westward and re-found Siris unless the other Greeks were prepared to fight the decisive sea-battle against the invading Persians at

Salamis. Although in many instances the particular occasion of the colony as described by the historians may be no more than an individual expression of a basic economic factor, a number of settlements must nevertheless have been made *ad hoc,* and for *ad hoc* reasons.

TRADE

It is often assumed that the growth of trade made it desirable for cities to establish colonies as markets for their goods. But such an assumption takes too sophisticated a view of ancient trade and of the attitude of ancient governments towards it. These, less paternal in this respect than those of modern times and fiscally less grasping (because they were content to leave everything except war to private enterprise), did not look on the trade of their citizens as a factor that could legitimately lead to political commitments in its support. Trading profit to a government involved only the volume of traffic entering and leaving the city's own harbour and the amount of goods, of whatever origin, sold in its own market. Finds of Corinthian pottery, for example, argue nothing as to the nationality of the trader who brought them or the origin of his ship, and are made in colonies other than those of Corinthian foundation. It was of course useful for mariners to have a friendly Greek city as a port of call, but in the west only Syracuse was the colony of a 'great trading city', and it is noteworthy that sites with good harbours likely to be of use for trade and hardly to be missed if that were the object, were not settled. Brindisi is a notable example. Conversely, many flourishing cities had poor harbours. Even in the cases of Ischia and Cumae, where it has been particularly suggested that some commercial motive may have intervened, this may only be a polite way of saying that they were well sited for piracy on a city-state scale, levying tolls on traders who needed to pass that way; for there too the harbours were not good, and the settlements are better accounted for as agricultural in basis.

The West was not the only area of Greek expansion in these

centuries. The Greeks settled in the northern Aegean, the sea of Marmora (*Propontis*), the Black (*Euxine*) Sea and the coast of Cyrenaica, and everywhere they carried with them their ideas and institutions. Yet in the western Mediterranean they flourished most, and by the accident of history and geography it was these colonies which have had the deepest effect on posterity. After the great impetus the colonising rush died down: subsequent colonies were often political in conception, and land-shortage began to find other remedies. In the West itself later foundations were colonies of the original settlements, and reflect the prosperity or disharmony which these had managed to achieve. By 600 B.C., at least as far as Sicily and Italy were concerned, old Greece had to all intents and purposes ended its colonising activity.

How and when the various colonies were founded, what happened to them, and what now survives for the modern traveller to see—at any rate as far as concerns the most significant remains—the pages that follow will try to describe.

THE EARLIEST COLONIES

It might have been expected that the pattern of colonisation would be one of settlement of the nearest suitable sites first, with a subsequent expansion using these as *points d'appui.* But the colonists aimed for the most desirable choice irrespective of distance. The earliest colonies were in fact the most northerly on the western seaboard of Italy, and the bay of Naples remained the farthest point of direct Greek penetration in this area. No doubt the Greeks had already gained experience of the regions concerned on trading journeys, although it is not clear how much direct trade is to be supposed before the first foundation. They may also have had in mind the Etruscan market and the metal trade, but a combination of security and availability of land seems to have been the main consideration.

ISCHIA

The island of Ischia, which the Greeks called Pithecussae, was ideal for their purposes. It was reasonably fertile and easily defensible, gold was said to be found there, and it was a good base for the levying of tolls on passing commerce which the settlers doubtless contemplated. Livy and Strabo mention specifically that its foundation preceded that of Cumae on the mainland, and that the colonists came from Chalcis and Eretria on the Greek island of Euboea. Despite their co-operation in colonising ventures, the differences between these two neighbour-cities resulted in warfare which, in the eighth or seventh century, involved many Greek states. This apparently had its repercussions in the west, for in consequence of discord the Eretrians had to abandon Pithecussae; but notwithstanding their success the Chalcidian victors did not prosper, and earthquakes and volcanic activity recommended their evacuation also. Probably Etruscan sea-power had added to their difficulties, and the mainland settlements, once established, made Ischia of less advantage and profit as a base.

Discoveries in the colonists' cemetery at Lacco Ameno leave no doubt that the ancient authors are right about the early date of the settlement, and the relationship of the material with pre-settlement tombs of Cumae suggests that Ischia's traditional precedence is also well-founded. Pottery fragments include much material of the late Geometric period, and form a continuous series through the Protocorinthian and Corinthian styles. That this evidence apparently comes to an end in the sixth century offers confirmation of Strabo's statement that the settlement was abandoned.

Among the complete or almost complete vases of the earliest period is a cup with a message scratched on it to the effect that anyone who drinks of it will be fired with the flames of Aphrodite. Possibly the earliest example yet discovered of Greek alphabetic writing, it also shows the writer's tolerable ability as a versifier and knowledge of the Homeric legends; for he

Plate 6

suggests that Nestor's cup is not to be compared with his. This cup is of an East Greek type, and Ischia, like Cumae in the early stages, provided a focus for exports not only from Corinth but also from the wider Aegean area. Later, Corinthian exports established a virtual monopoly. A foundation date for the colony somewhere towards the middle of the eighth century B.C. would not do violence to the evidence, and implies that soon after the first Olympiad the Greek *poleis* were settled enough for the organisation of colonising expeditions on a co-operative basis.

CUMAE

It was, however, Ischia's neighbour Cumae which was to play so important a part as a channel for the influence of Hellas on the west. The Cumaean graves have proved a rich source for the comparative study of pottery of the eighth, seventh and sixth centuries, and emphasise Corinthian domination of the market in fine ware for most of that time. The conclusion again appears to be that the settlement was established between *c.*750 and 725 B.C., although Greek imports had even before that become familiar to the existing population. Livy says that Cumae was colonised from Ischia: at any rate its colonists were predominantly Euboean in origin. Here too a *graffito* has provided a very early example of Greek writing—this time on a Protocorinthian *aryballos* of a type datable to the first quarter of the seventh century. 'I am Tataie's *lekythos*,' wrote its owner; 'may anyone who steals me be struck blind.' That the Latin

Fig. 4a–c

Fig. 4. a and b. Protocorinthian aryballoi found at Cumae, early seventh century B.C. Height of a, *5.7 cm., of* b, *5.5 cm. Aryballos* b *is the 'lekythos of Tataie'*
c. Tataie's inscription

alphabet was a derivative of the Greek is well known: but Tataie, like the owner of the Ischia cup, used an alphabet peculiar to the Euboeans. It was this alphabet that the Etruscans learned when they made contact with this outpost of Hellenism, and from them it spread to the Romans. On a gold *fibula* from Praeneste is inscribed one of the earliest extant examples of Latin, and this makes use of characters recognisably akin to those of Tataie. It can hardly have been written very much later than hers. It may be added that the Hellenic elements which began to affect the native Roman religion also seem to have filtered through from direct or indirect Cumaean contacts.

Plate 5

Cumae is said to have owed its name to Cyme in Aeolis, which joined in the foundation; and the participation of the Graei from central Greece may have had the chance result that the Romans were led to refer to the whole colony (and hence to the people from whom it sprang) as 'Graeci'. Its position emphasises the defensive considerations which were allied to the need for additional lands; it had no good harbour—only an open beach—and better agricultural possibilities were available elsewhere in the neighbourhood. It had, however, a useful acropolis dominating the shore, and was protected on the north by the Lago di Liccola, while to the east the mountains made attack difficult. At a later date Dicaearchia (*Pozzuoli*), a Samian foundation on the other side of Capo Miseno, was acquired to supply the harbour Cumae lacked, and Parthenope, refounded by the Cumaeans under the name Neapolis (*Naples*), soon eclipsed its parent-city.

CONTACT WITH ETRURIA

There was also some assimilation to the neighbouring Etruscan power. Jewellery found at Cumae has been interpreted as showing not only imports from Etruria but Etruscan craftsmen at work in the city itself. Politically also there was a period of *rapprochement* with the Etruscans: but when Etruscan expansion pressed hard on the Cumaeans their resistance was worthy of that shown by their compatriots elsewhere against barbarian attack. In 524 B.C., 4,500 Cumaeans under Aristodemus routed a large Etruscan army in a battle in which the city's natural defences played an important part. But growing emphasis on trade meant that Cumaean interests extended beyond the immediate confines of the bay of Naples, and the participation of Cumaeans in the foundation of Zancle, the later Messana, shows that the safeguarding of the route to Greece formed a cardinal element of their politics.

The power of Cumae declined in the later fifth century, so that it fell under the domination of the Samnites, and during the fourth it passed, like the Samnites themselves, into the dominion of Rome, with Naples becoming the chief city of the region; but its rôle as the initial mediator of Greek civilisation to the west cannot be overemphasised. The tourist who visits the cave of the Virgilian Sibyl stands on ground more important for the development of the western world than he may perhaps realise.

NAXOS

Thucydides says that the first Greek colony in Sicily was founded at Naxos, that its settlers came from Chalcis in Euboea, and that their organiser-in-chief (*oikistes*) was named Thucles. Other sources add settlers from the Aegean island of Naxos, and thus explain the city's name, but the tradition seems doubtful. From Thucydides' chronology we gather that he believed the settlement to have taken place (on our reckoning) in 735–4 B.C. The altar to 'Apollo the Leader' which Thucles established was held in particular veneration by all the Sicilian Greeks, and ambassadors who left the island for religious gatherings in Greece sacrificed on it in the course of their journey.

It is not possible on present evidence to judge to what extent eastern Sicily was already well known to the Greeks. Possibly earlier contacts of trade or exploration had put them on good terms with its Sicel inhabitants. At least, while Naxos and its subsequent daughter-foundations flourished, the Sicels continued to live unmolested and unmolesting in the neighbourhood. The site of Naxos, on the promontory of Capo Schisò, was possibly chosen as the first landfall dictated by the course of a ship crossing from Capo Spartivento. If the configuration of the land was much the same then as now, it had a small but useful harbour protected by the promontory; and it commanded the valley of the river Alcantara, itself well defended by the north side of Mt Etna and by the barrier of the Nebrodi and Peloritani mountains. Naxos was thus the key to the whole area, a base for wider colonisation, rather than a compact strongpoint such as we have seen Ischia and Cumae to be. The fertile possibilities of the Etna region for permanent agricultural settlement must have been a primary consideration when it was decided to send the colony out.

Plate 7

This seems to be confirmed by the number of the settlers, and it is evident that this was to be a major outlet for the surplus population of Euboea. Within six years of Naxos' foundation, Thucles led a party southwards to take possession of the site of Leontini (*Lentini*), on the hills looking northward over the rich plain of the Simeto. The intervening region was soon afterwards secured by the settlement of Catana (*Catania*) under the *oikistes* Evarchus. This site had the triple advantage of commanding a good harbour, of controlling the southern slopes of Etna and the plain to the south, and of guarding the route towards Centuripae, Enna and other native communities in the interior of the island. Leontini similarly commanded the road to the modern Caltagirone, which has provided considerable Sicel material and was clearly an important native centre. Thus trade and security, as well as the territorial needs of a permanent agricultural colony, were amply served in the choice of both sites.

This being so, it looks as if Naxos' function was primarily that of a stepping-stone. Its site though attractive is not well defensible and remained small. It was formerly thought that all evidence of the city had vanished utterly, but parts of the circuit-walls have recently been uncovered and the whole course of them traced. It has also become clear not only that the site was inhabited before the Chalcidians came but also that the tradition of Naxos' destruction by Dionysius of Syracuse in 402 B.C. must be looked at anew. A street following a revised city layout seems to belong to the fourth century, and grave deposits continue to the Hellenistic period. Of Naxos' history, culminating in this destruction and the foundation of Tauromenium (*Taormina*) on the hill above the bay, more will be said later: but it remained without strength of its own, and was uncomfortably situated in the rivalry between Syracuse and Messana.

Plate 8

SYRACUSE

A year after the foundation of Naxos, Thucydides' account continues, the Corinthian Archias led a colony of his countrymen to the site of Syracuse, where they settled on the island of Ortygia after having driven out the Sicels who were already in possession. Legend subsequently gathered round the founder's name: Plutarch, for instance, has a moving story of a love-affair and its unhappy consequences, as a result of which Apollo at Delphi ordered Archias into the exile of colony-making. It may be doubted whether at so early a date the Delphic oracle was important enough to be responsible for this or any other foundation; but its later importance magnified its place in the tradition, and it perhaps became a source of information on potential sites which it was advisable to consult before colonists were sent out.

Syracuse quickly grew and prospered, and became the greatest city of Sicily: so much so that its history becomes in effect the history of the whole island, and most of chapter IV will revolve round it. The most notable of its Greek buildings still survive, and the philhellene traveller finds it one of his most attractive ports of call. The view from the top of the theatre or from Euryalus shows clearly the advantages of the site—a large,

Plate 41

calm harbour with a comparatively narrow entrance (less than a mile across), the island of Ortygia (soon joined to the mainland by a causeway) which formed a natural and easily defensible acropolis, a smaller harbour on the seaward side, a good northern defence-line along the ridge of Epipolae, and a large fertile plain along the shore to Avola and Pachino, extending inland up the Anapo and Cassibile valleys towards Palazzolo Acreide and Monte Lauro. On the landward side of the Great Harbour lay marshes which more than once, by encouraging sickness among besieging armies, saved the city when all seemed lost. Apart from that, the climate was as favourable as the situation, and we have Cicero's word for it that no day passes in Syracuse without sunshine. Cicero, who served as a junior administrator at the opposite end of the island in Lilybaeum (*Marsala*), had a warm affection for the city which animates his lyrical description (IV *Verr.* 52–3) of its beauty and splendour.

EXPANSION OF SYRACUSE

The original settlers each received an allotment of the plain country, and as the population increased they became an aristocratic *élite* known as *Gamoroi* ('land-participants'). In the seventh century what little is known of Syracusan history indicates both growth and unrest. Expansion up the Anapo valley resulted *c.* 663 B.C. in the foundation of Acrae (*Palazzolo Acreide*), and at about the same time the family of Myletidae was expelled—a group numerous enough to play an important part in the foundation of Himera on the north coast. Later in the century internal trouble seems to have brought about some modification in what must have originally been a close oligarchical government, and during the century following things apparently became quieter.

See p. 55

In fact, in the sixth century archaic Syracuse seems to have been at its most flourishing. The temple of Apollo is of this date, as is the temple of Olympian Zeus among the orange groves on the far side of the Great Harbour. A temple of

Athena of the same period was rebuilt a hundred years later, but the site has produced evidence of a number of archaic sanctuary buildings and a quantity of painted terracotta decoration belonging to them. Meanwhile the inhabited area quickly outgrew Ortygia and spread to the district beyond the causeway known as Achradina.

In south-eastern Sicily Syracusan domination became more marked. The settlements of Casmenae (*Monte Casale,* west of Acrae) *c.* 643 B.C. and of Camarina (598 B.C.), at the mouth of the river Hipparis south-west of the modern Vittoria, formed the basis for a steady penetration of the whole upland area of which more will be said in the next section. Further Syracusan expansion in this direction was blocked by the territory of Gela, and this was a matter for a later generation to resolve.

MEGARA HYBLAEA

To the north, in the plain beyond the broad ridge of Epipolae, lay the settlement of Megara Hyblaea. This site, scarcely 25 kilometres from Syracuse, was founded, according to the tradition, five years later than the Corinthian colony. Its settlers came from Corinth's neighbour Megara, and on their first arrival in Sicily found themselves in difficulties because the likely territory had already been pre-empted by Syracuse and Leontini. They settled at Trotilon (near *Brucoli,* north of Augusta), where they made themselves a nuisance to the Leontines, with the result that the latter tried to absorb them into their own community: but this arrangement did not succeed, and after a brief spell at Thapsus (*Magnisi*), where their *oikistes* Lamis died, the Megarians settled on the plain below Melilli, the Sicel town of Hybla, whose king gave them the land. Megara Hyblaea's existence thus depended on good relations with the Sicels, and in the early period the city seems to have maintained a precarious independence of Syracuse. Orsi long ago discovered part of its walls and cemetery, and his initial work has more recently been resumed and expanded by Villard and Vallet. To the remains of an archaic temple identified by

Orsi they have added the traces of a second, together with sufficient elements of a simpler and smaller shrine to enable a reconstruction to be suggested. All these buildings were destroyed by the Syracusans in 483–2 B.C.; the fortifications now to be seen belong to a third-century revival which the Romans, at the time of their great siege of Syracuse, brought to an abrupt end.

Fig. 5

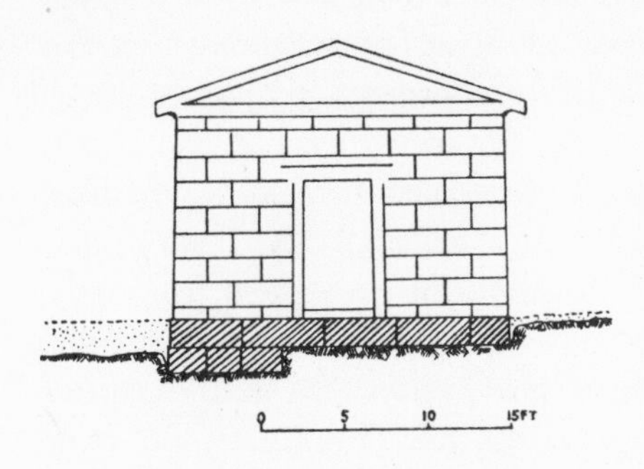

Fig. 5. Main entry of small archaic temple at Megara Hyblaea, redrawn from the restoration by F. Villard and G. Vallet. To be dated between 510 and 483 B.C., it measured some 14 by 7 m. but was not quite rectangular

THE SICILIAN COLONIES

The initial ventures of the Euboeans, Corinthians and Megarians made the other Greeks alive to the possibilities Sicily offered. It is a larger island than is often casually supposed; its mountains though formidable prove no insuperable obstacles to the settler or invader, and though they canalise access they do not frustrate it. Natural defensive lines are thus few, and in later times warfare could and did swing rapidly from one end of Sicily to the other. Wide areas of plain, as around Catania, Gela and Marsala, and fertile upland valleys meant that corn and olive could alike flourish, while the hills offered ample possibilities for the pasturage of sheep and goats. The lush spring and arid, dusty summer reproduced, like the landscape, what was already familiar to the Greeks, yet on a more generous scale. Thus Sicily, 'quest'America dell'antichità' as Tomasi di Lampedusa justly described it, called to the Greek settlers, and the Greeks came.

PATTERN OF GREEK SETTLEMENT

It was settlement rather than trade that was their object. Greek imports in native sites do not clearly precede the Greek foundations; rather; it seems, are they at their earliest contemporary with them, and the trade which developed was more in locally-made Greek ware than in pottery of Greek origin for which the colonies served as entrepôts. Nevertheless, vases from the home country continued to be a popular import for the colonists themselves. In all their colonising activity they generally preferred to keep close to the sea, their highroad and if need be their lifeline. Inland settlements were few, and even then usually depended on the firm base of a coastal city. Their principal colonies thus formed a fringe around the eastern and southern coasts of the the island. The north coast they found more difficult of access, and the far west, as will be seen, remained closed to their settlement save in a single instance. In the centre of Sicily, already thickly settled by the pre-Greek inhabitants, Hellenic influence steadily expanded into a more or less effective domination. The course of excavation has tended to disprove a picture of a Greek coastline and a backward native interior. Morgantina, in the very centre of the island, was a Hellenised city in the archaic period, and by the early fifth century a thoroughgoing intermarriage of Hellenic and local influences had taken place, at least in the inhabited centres. That a strong national feeling survived outside these localities is nevertheless apparent from events later in that century.

The state of Sicilian culture before the Greeks came has been well described by L. Bernabò Brea in his study *Sicily before the Greeks,* and need not be discussed here. Thucydides refers to three native elements, the Elymians, the Sicans and the Sicels.

ELYMIANS

Of these, the Elymians lived in the west, in the region south and west of Palermo. Their continuing political independence left them none the less receptive to Hellenic influences, and their main centres, Segesta, Halicyae (*Salemi*), Eryx (*Erice*) and Entella (*Rocca d'Entella*) developed something of a city life on the Greek pattern. The more important, Segesta and Halicyae, entered during the fifth century into close diplomatic relations with Athens, which had far-reaching consequences. At Segesta, one of the most picturesque of all Sicilian sites, the peristyle of an unfinished Doric temple testifies to the fifth-century inhabitants' pretensions, and the theatre on the neighbouring hill, overlooking the noble blue crescent of the Golfo di Castellamare, emphasises their determination to become as Greek as the Greeks. No less Hellenic was the bitterness of their international rivalries, and the mutual antagonism of Segestaeans and Selinuntines was a permanent factor in Sicilian politics until the destruction of Selinus by the Carthaginians in 409 B.C.

Plate 9

Plate 10

CARTHAGINIANS

The interest of Carthage in the island was natural for so close a neighbour (on a good day Cape Bon is visible from Erice), but, as elsewhere, the Carthaginians were content to establish emporia rather than to embark on conquest. These more serious ambitions emerge later—first in 480 B.C. and intermittently thereafter until the final Roman victory. In the archaic period they confined themselves to three settlements, Panormus (*Palermo*), Soloeis (*Solunto*) and the island of Motya near Marsala. This part of the island, as a result, though absorbing Greek influences was never Greek in any direct sense.

SICANS AND SICELS

The Sicans and Sicels, on the other hand, were more exposed to Greek penetration and frequently in the path of the Greeks' inter-state warfare. The river Gelas seems to have been the boundary between these two peoples, and while the Sicels appear from the tradition (and from the archaeology) the more pacific, literary evidence suggests that both Gela and Acragas were faced with Sican wars. Only once, in the mid-fifth century, did the Sicels develop any national unity; otherwise they showed varying degrees of acceptance, voluntary or enforced, of

Greek domination, which are perhaps best to be described by using as a context the southernmost area of the island and the stages of Hellenism which it underwent.

SYRACUSE AND THE SOUTH

Syracusan penetration of this region followed the lines of the routes to Acrae and Casmenae in the west and Helorus in the south, and Camarina acted as an independent coastal base. A route through Hybla Heraea (*Ragusa*) and Còmiso linked Casmenae and Camarina. Hybla was a Sicel town, but sixth-century material found in tombs there has led archaeologists to suppose that it contained a Greek commercial element. Definite Greek settlement, however, does not seem to have taken place either along this route or along the alternative (followed by the modern road) via Ispica and Modica. The main road towards the plain of Gela led from Acrae to Acrillae (*Chiaramonte Gulfi*), where a Syracusan staging-post seems to have been organised in the sixth century. A settlement by the river Dirillo at Scornavacche, destroyed in the early fifth century, contains Greek evidence belonging at the earliest to the first half of the sixth, which further illustrates the importance of this road for trade and invasion. By contrast, however, a native settlement at Castiglione (between Ragusa and Còmiso) although accepting Greek imports seems to have shown remarkable resistance to Hellenisation until it also was destroyed in the early fifth century. Camarina revolted against the domination of its parent-city about 550 B.C. and in the war which ended in the colony's destruction the Sicels are named among its allies: the Greeks of Gela, though in alliance with the Camarinaeans, apparently opted out of the war.

The pattern of Greek penetration which emerges is thus uneven. A strong hold was kept on the westward road, and there was substantial infiltration by means of commerce into the principal Sicel settlements, but outside these the pace of Hellenisation was slower. Sicel resistance in this area may be partly due to bad relations with the Syracusans from the time of

Archias's foundation. In founding his colony he had destroyed the existing Sicel settlement, and Sicels were used as serf-labour on the estates of the *Gamoroi.* In addition, the Syracusans already perhaps cherished political ambitions not shared by the other settlers. 'Syracuse', wrote T. J. Dunbabin, 'was marked out from its origin for rule among the cities of Sicily.' It appears that the Syracusans, even in the sixth century, were conscious of their destiny.

It will have become apparent that the Sicilian colonies may be divided into two groups—primary colonies founded directly from Greece, such as Naxos, Syracuse and Megara Hyblaea, and secondary colonies founded as offshoots of these, of which Leontini, Catana and Camarina have provided examples. In some cases these secondary foundations eclipsed their parents in wealth and importance. This was certainly so with the Naxian colonies, although archaeology can show little of their prosperity. Catana has suffered too severely from man and nature for much to have survived from antiquity, although a recently discovered and rich pottery deposit, with material of the seventh to the fourth century, is likely to provide valuable new evidence. The code of laws drawn up for it by the law-giver Charondas served as a model for other cities and shows that its early constitution was aristocratic. It may have sent a further offshoot to a settlement near Randazzo, and it certainly had an influence on, and no doubt close relations with, the Sicels of Adrano and Paternò. The latter in particular became very Hellenised, and the pattern of settlement and influence in this region confirms that already described for the south. The same holds good for Leontini. The Leontines had perhaps a less successful Sicel relationship, and after an initial period of co-operation expelled the Sicels from their territory. But the surrounding territory, as evidence from sites such as Scordia and Grammichele shows, saw a gradual Hellenisation of the independent Sicels within the Leontine orbit. It was at one time

CATANA

thought that the Emperor Frederick II (1194–1250) in building Augusta had carried off all that remained of ancient Leontini, but excavation by Orsi and latterly under the direction of G. Rizza has revealed part of the wall, with the Syracuse gate, the earliest phase of which goes back to the sixth century. The position and prosperity of Leontini gave it more chance than Megara had of withstanding Syracusan expansion, and enmity between the two cities was responsible for much warfare and misery in the fifth century. Thereafter, Leontini became more or less a Syracusan dependency.

For Megara Hyblaea expansion and growth of influence in the immediate neighbourhood was impossible. There is literary evidence of warfare against Leontini at the end of the seventh century, and Megara appears as an ally of Syracuse in the war against Camarina. It was thus already within the orbit of its destroyer. But in its comparatively short career of independence it sent out one colony of its own, and that an important one. Thucydides dates it one hundred years after Megara's own foundation, and adds that an *oikistes* was, in accordance with custom, sought from the parent-city in Greece. This leader, Pammilus, looked for a suitable site on the south coast beyond Gela, and found it far to the west at Selinus (*Selinunte*), on the edge of Elymian and Carthaginian territory. Here also was a wide area for agricultural development between the hills and the sea, especially to the west, and in this direction a guard post at Mazare (*Mazzara del Vallo*) marked the Selinuntine frontier. Eastwards beyond Sciacca their boundary marched with that of the Geloan foundation of Acragas, while to the north their relations with the Elymians were always uneasy. As the most westerly outpost of Hellas in Sicily, Selinus was in a precarious situation and suffered from it. Furthermore, the site of the city though impressive and with a well-defended acropolis had no natural strength. It lay on an open coast with no harbour save the shelter, to the west of the acropolis, of the

SELINUS

Fig. 6

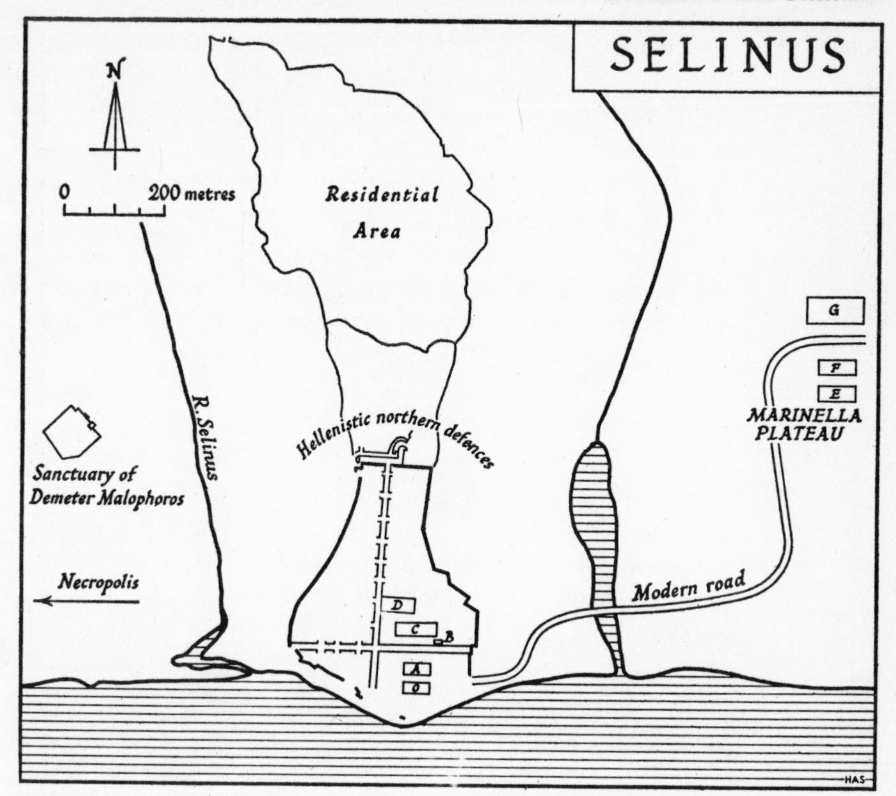

Fig. 6

mouth of the river Selinus from which, with its luxuriant growth of wild parsley (*selinon*), the city derived its name. A depression to the east, also supposed to have been a harbour of some kind, divided the acropolis from the plateau now called Marinella: the principal inhabited quarter lay on higher ground behind the acropolis, and had no defences.

The Selinuntines in their western isolation needed the gods' aid, and were apparently soon rich enough to pay for it. The size and splendour of their temples can only have been the product of swift and considerable prosperity. Of these temples

Plates 12, 13

three (usually designated E, F and G, in the absence of certain knowledge of the gods to whom they were dedicated), were set apart on the Marinella plateau, while the others (A, C, D, O and the small B) stood on the acropolis itself. The visitor to Selinus readily feels, with Bérard, *l'impression émouvante* created by the complete destruction of these great buildings ('les squelettes géants des temples selinuntins')—a devastation so thorough that in a pre-atomic age nothing but an earthquake could have achieved it. The recent rebuilding of much of temples C and E diminishes but does not destroy the effect.

The complexity of the ruins and the size of the architectural elements discouraged early archaeologists, but in the nineteenth century three well-known metopes from the earliest of the temples (C, of *c.* 550 B.C.) and four from temple F (mid-fifth century) were taken to Palermo museum. Both groups have held, ever since, an important place in the history of Greek sculpture: allowances must be made for provincialism, but the later set shows a certain grace and the earlier lively good humour.

Plate 11

An archaic metope showing the rape of Europa belongs to a temple dismembered to make way for a more elaborate successor. The cornices of temple C, in painted terra-cotta, now reconstructed in the same museum, are among the most notable of those surviving from the archaic period and have made a particular contribution to the study of this aspect of early Greek architecture, so well exemplified in the west. Also important architecturally is the sanctuary of Demeter Malophoros on the far side of the river Selinus in the locality called Gaggera. Here a complex of buildings has been excavated the principal among which, the 'Megaron' (*c.* 575 B.C.), had peculiarities of cornice and roof construction. It was a plain building, with no encircling colonnade, but the popularity of the sanctuary is attested by the great number of dedicatory figurines found there. The extensive necropolis, also the source of a wealth of 'small finds', lay like the Malophoros sanctuary beyond the river. The residential quarter on the acropolis is later in date than the destruction of 409. The rectangular street-plan on which it is arranged has been attributed to the sixth century, but the argument has been challenged. Nevertheless the parallel case of Acragas suggests that it is not necessarily unwise to credit the western Greeks with the use of this 'Hippodamian' scheme, a century before Hippodamus is said to have invented it. The fortifications also belong to this restoration-period, and at the northern end their complex arrangement makes the best of a poor natural situation.

GELA

Of Gela we are told that it was founded forty-five years after Syracuse, that like Selinus it took its name from the river at the mouth of which it lay, and that it had two *oikistai,* Antiphemus of Rhodes and Entimus of Crete. This intervention broke the virtual Euboean-Corinthian monopoly of Sicilian colonisation and as an example of inter-state co-operation is even more noteworthy than that between Chalcis and Eretria. The Rhodian element seems to have prevailed and Antiphemus alone to have been the object of the founder-cult. The acropolis, nostalgically named Lindioi (*Molino a vento*), was no doubt the point of first settlement, but ultimately the city occupied the whole of a low ridge some 2 kilometres long—an extent which the growing modern town is just beginning to fill—overlooking the wide though comparatively shallow plain and without any real harbour. Its natural defensive position was reinforced at the late-fourth-century restoration by a magnificent circuit of fortifications, the westernmost section of which, disinterred from the sand-dunes of Capo Soprano, is among the most impressive of surviving Greek defence-works. Apart from that, little remains above ground of ancient Gela. One column of a sixth-century Doric temple stands at Molino a vento, the east end of the ridge, near the museum which itself covers the site of at least two early treasuries. Excavations at this point have confirmed the existence of a cult of Demeter, and have produced substantial fragments of the painted terracotta revetments of the

Plate 46

shrines with which the numerous figurines were associated. Terracotta antefixes in the form of grotesque yet kindly satyr-heads deserve special mention as lively evidence of the skill and quality of Geloan coroplastic art in the fifth century. Gela seems indeed to have been a principal centre for the manufacture of architectural and votive terracottas, and examples found in other contexts may be Geloan in origin.

Plate 14

THE GELOAN HINTERLAND

To the east the river Dirillo seems to have been the boundary between Gela and Camarina, and marked the limit of Syracusan expansion. Northwards, although there is a tradition of warfare, penetration of the hill-country and native settlements seems to have been continuous and effective. At Monte Saraceno near Ravanusa remains of an early sixth-century temple and archaic treasuries have been found, and votive deposits are even earlier in date. As far inland as Vassallaggi near Caltanissetta a native centre was fully Hellenised by the middle of the sixth century, while at Butera, an important settlement easily visible from Capo Soprano, the same process was completed at a very early stage. The bulk of the pottery for the Geloan inland trade was locally made: its styles sometimes echoed and sometimes diverged widely from those of the settlers' Aegean homes. But, as in the other colonies, there was a constant flow of pottery from Greece to and through Gela, and the growing evidence suggests that the settlement quickly reached a very high level of prosperity and influence.

Plates 15, 16

That the Geloans quickly expanded their territories westward is shown not only by the Megarians' careful avoidance of the whole tract between Gela and Sciacca in their foundation of Selinus but also by the evidence of early settlement at Licata and Palma di Montechiaro. This expansion in the seventh century was crowned in the sixth by the establishment of a new colony destined to be larger and more important than Gela itself. Acragas lies on the slope of a hill some 5 kilometres inland from the sea: the residential section of the city was almost

ACRAGAS

encircled by a protecting ridge which, rising high to the north-east, provided a strong acropolis now covered by modern Agrigento. That part of the ridge which lay between the city and the sea housed many of the major Acragantine religious sanctuaries, and it is the imposing line of temples strung out along it, in varying degrees of preservation, which is the chief Acragantine legacy to posterity.

The settlement of Acragas in 580 and its rapid development thereafter provide a clear case in which colonisation and land-occupation rather than trade were the motivating factor. Even though a harbour is given a passing mention by Strabo, it had no good port, nor ever did so until Porto Empedocle was built, partly from Acragantine material, during the eighteenth century. On the other hand the abundance of its agricultural products is much emphasised by the ancient writers, and on this the bulk of a population which is said to have reached a figure of almost a quarter of a million must have depended. The original settlement was presumably confined to the acropolis, but it rapidly spread. The excavation of a Hellenistic and Roman residential quarter near the church of S. Nicolò has recently shown that the earliest structures on the site belong to the sixth century, and here as at Selinus it is possible that a 'grid-iron' plan was already in use. What is more, the great circuit-wall, linking the acropolis, the sanctuary of Demeter to the east, and the main line of temples to the south, seems to have been laid out in the middle of the same century.

PHALARIS OF ACRAGAS

The whole sudden upsurge of Acragantine prosperity may be associated with the shadowy and traditionally unpleasant autocrat Phalaris, whose reign seems to have lasted from *c.* 565 to *c.* 549. His name is linked with successful warfare against the Sicans and with the establishment of Acragas' eastern boundary close by Licata. The truth about his cruelty in general, and in particular of the roasting of victims in the famous brazen bull (a story already current in the early fifth century), lies concealed beneath an embroidery of legend and was a debated subject among the ancient historians of Sicily. His sixteen-year reign ended in assassination, but his ruthless violence was a fitting prelude to the history of a city which, despite its wealth, endured repeated misery, slaughter and oppression.

Fig. 8
Plate 18

Apart from the temple of Olympian Zeus and the precinct of the chthonic divinities to the west of it, it is not known what deities are to be associated with the various sanctuaries of Acragas. The early-fifth-century temple underlying the church of S. Biagio is probably that of Demeter, and a temple of Zeus on the acropolis, which Phalaris is said to have built, lies beneath the church of S. Gerlando. The city was hailed by Pindar as 'the seat of Persephone', and to this cult two archaic sanctuaries have been attributed. He also salutes it as 'most beautiful of mortal cities, that lives upon the hill of fine dwellings, above the banks where the sheep graze beside the river.' Though in his day many of the surviving monuments were as yet unbuilt, and though in ours much that was beautiful and fine has been irretrievably lost, Pindar was, we may still feel, not far wrong.

Plate 17

HERACLEA MINOA

Plate 19

A Selinuntine colony, on a lonely and attractive stretch of coast some 25 kilometres west of Acragas at the mouth of the river Platani, was doubtless a response to the growing power of the Acragantines. Originally called Minoa, it received at some uncertain date the additional name Heraclea, first clearly attested in 314 B.C. Captured by Euryleon before his attempt on Selinus, it fell into Acragantine hands before the end of the sixth century. Excavations have begun to reveal more of what was until recently a little-known site, but the theatre, stretch of city-wall and remains of private houses so far disinterred belong to the fourth century and later. Small finds, however, have reflected the earliest stage of Heraclean history.

See p. 74

ZANCLE

Of the north coast of Sicily little need be said. The eastern end was dominated by Zancle (*Messina*), so named from a native word meaning 'sickle', and describing the shape of the harbour. Zancle's history was chequered. The original foundation (in the eighth century but later than Naxos) by colonists from Cumae whom tradition called 'pirates' was followed by resettlement from Euboea under the *oikistai* Perieres and Crataemenes. Repeated destruction has left little trace of the archaic city—no more than a few vases imported from Greece, the earliest of which, however, serve to confirm the suggested date of foundation. Its position had a strategic and commercial rather than an agricultural value, and Zanclaean policy was of necessity directed to ensuring that the people of Rhegium on the opposite coast were well disposed, and that the more abundant agricultural land provided by the northern coastal strip was available to them. Thus they contributed an *oikistes* (Antimnestus) and settlers when the Euboeans found Rhegium, and by themselves at an early date they colonised the site of Mylae (*Milazzo*). Beyond this point they may have found resistance too strong: the mountains keep close to the sea all along the coast and give little foothold or room for expansion. Sites such as Tyndaris and Cephaloedium (*Cefalù*) were not settled until the fourth century, when the Hellenisation of the island was already at an advanced stage. Only at Himera, between Cefalù and Palermo, did a Zanclaean settlement succeed. Founded, according to Diodorus, in 648, it included the exiled Myletidae from Syracuse and perhaps a contingent from Euboea. The valley of the river Himeras gave it a reasonable amount of arable land, but it remained small and isolated in hostile territory. Its lack of natural advantages has led to the suggestion that it was intended to supplant Panormus as a way-station for trade with Spain. As the site of Gelon's great victory in 480, it acquired like Plataea a special fame which led to its undoing, and its destruction by the Carthaginians in 408 has left only the remains of the great temple which had commemorated their earlier defeat.

Plate 48

HIMERA

See p. 41

Plate 34

THE ITALIAN COLONIES

Although the Greeks were establishing colonies in southern Italy during the same period in which they were colonising Sicily, the problems they encountered and the pattern of development there were very different. Euboea, Corinth and to a lesser extent Megara, Rhodes and Crete had provided colonists for Sicily. In Italy the main impetus came from Achaea, the northern coastal strip of the Peloponnese, with support from such diverse sources as Locris, Sparta and Troezen, and, from as far away as Asia Minor, Colophon and Phocaea. The insularity of Sicily and the comparative ease of land communication had made it possible for the Greeks to establish a general control and to implant their influence firmly in the new territory. In southern Italy the mountain barriers are strong, and the inland fastnesses were difficult to influence in peace or conquer in war, while the communications along the coast on both sides of the Calabrian peninsula were so poor as to keep the Greek cities more isolated from each other. Finally, the native inhabitants were of a very different calibre. Tough and resilient, the Bruttians and Lucanians fought back against Greek attempts to dominate their territory, and though to some extent they absorbed Greek material culture they turned the tables politically on their would-be conquerors. Most of the Greek settlements had been ruined by their warfare with each other and with the Italian tribes before the ultimate conquest of them all by Rome.

The Adriatic coast of Italy had no interest for the colonisers, despite Greek commercial contacts with the Etruscans through emporia such as Spina and Hadria at the mouth of the river Po. Spina has in recent years been particularly prolific in discoveries of Attic vases of the sixth and fifth centuries which attest the volume of this trade, and as late as 325–4 B.C. the Athenians sent a colony to Hadria, though beyond the record of its despatch nothing is known of it. It is possible that the westward pattern set by the earliest colonies had a determining influence on subsequent colonial thought, for the coastline at any rate south of Monte Gargano presents no geographical difficulty to access or settlement. But for whatever reason, the whole area of Greek colonisation in Italy lay between the Gulf of Taranto and the bay of Naples. Settlement was haphazard, and like the seed that fell on stony ground the Greek cities rose swiftly to a luxuriant growth, which withered into no less swift a decline.

RHEGIUM

The earliest foundation of all was that at Rhegium (*Reggio di Calabria*), which has more in common with Sicily than with Italy. The solitary Euboean colony on the mainland south of Cumae, it aimed to secure the control of the straits for Zancle, to which it was the complement. The date of its foundation, which seems to follow quickly upon that of Zancle, is related to that of the Spartan conquest of Messenia, for a contingent of Messenians took part in the settlement and acquired the dominant voice in its affairs. Reggio, like Messana-Zancle, has been much devastated by earthquake, and little remains of the ancient city. An important cemetery beginning in the archaic period lay beneath the Museo Nazionale; fragments of the circuit wall have been discovered near the sea-front and, more recently, to to the north, while within their confines chance discoveries from time to time contribute to the shadowy picture. However, the sites of at least three sanctuaries are known, one of which lay beside the sea near the Museum and another below the Prefettura. These have yielded architectural terracotta fragments, votive figurines and vases of seventh-century date.

Backed by the inhospitable Aspromonte range, Rhegine territory could expand only along the shore. To the south its borders marched with those of Locri, and the modern Melito may lie at the boundary between the two: to the north Palmi or Gioia Tauro may mark the limit, here also imposed by Locrian dependencies. Metaurum, at the latter site, is said variously to have been founded from Zancle or from Locri. Despite their proximity, Rhegium and Locri seem to have maintained friendly relations in the archaic period, but these later deteriorated into an enmity only appeased by the destruction of Rhegium in 387 B.C. at the hands of the Locrians' Syracusan allies. Nevertheless the city was refounded, and flourished anew under the *pax Romana.*

LOCRI

The Locrian colonists had arrived when better sites along the Calabrian shore had already been occupied. The coast at this point is open and featureless, and inland the plain soon begins to rise up to the foothills of the Aspromonte. Arable territory was thus limited; although the circuit of the walls—strengthened here and there by massive towers—has been recognised, the harbour has so far escaped identification. The city was built on the north side of the fiumara di Portigliola, on three ridges running inland, together with the valleys between; the site rises quite sharply, and the acropolis lay at the furthest and highest point. The extant remains are scattered, and the best of the finds are now to be seen in the museum at Reggio. Among them is the magnificent horseman terracotta, reconstructed from fragments found at the site of a large late-sixth-century Doric temple a kilometre or so inland at the Casa Marafioti. As an akroterion it surmounted a building remarkable for the artistry of its terracotta cornice and for the replacement of the usual triglyphs with pentaglyphs in the frieze. Closer to the sea, in the area called Marasà, was one of the two* Ionic temples in western Greece, the fifth-century successor of two archaic shrines. It is doubtful whether this is to be associated with the famous sanctuary of Persephone, to whose cult belong the striking and well-executed series of terracotta plaques illustrating, for the most part, features of the legend or ritual of the goddess. Sicily and Magna Graecia, as has already

Plate 22
Fig. 7
Plate 20
Plate 21
Plate 79

* The other was at the Locrians' own colony Hipponium.

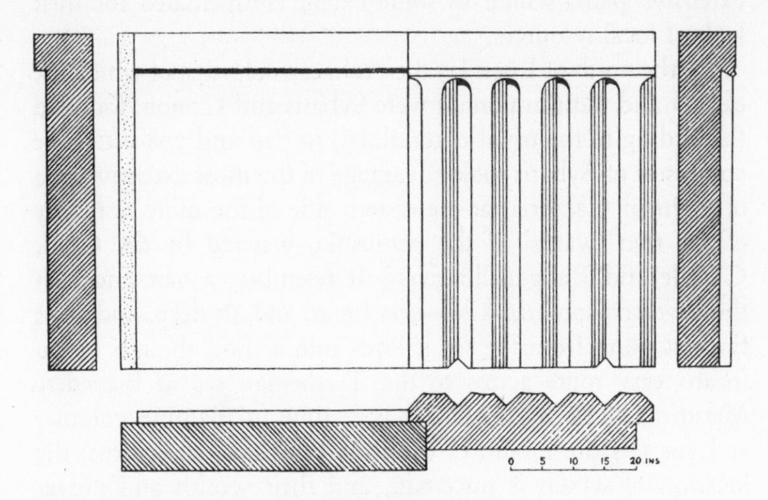

Fig. 7. Entablature of the Doric (Marafioti) temple, Locri

been noted, are in general rich in both quality and quantity of terracotta work: even so, that from Locri is unsurpassed.

From which part of Greek Locris the settlers came was hotly debated in antiquity. Founded with Syracusan help between 680 and 670 B.C. (though some would place it twenty years earlier), Locri could boast a code of laws drawn up by Zaleucus, the earliest of Greek law-givers, and this though severe was adopted by many other cities. Much legend later attached itself to Zaleucus' name: he had a great reputation as a political arbitrator, but the Locrian constitution was firmly aristocratic, power being concentrated in the hands of the so-called 'hundred families'. Under their administration the Locrians succeeded in extending their control through the Aspromonte mountains to the Tyrrhenian sea, controlling one of the best of the cross-routes (that through Taurianova) and founding colonies during the sixth century at Hipponium (*Vibo Valentia*) and Medma (*Rosarno*). This gave them command of a rich and extensive plain which to some extent compensated for their lack of local resources.

SYBARIS

To the north of Locri lay the Achaean colonies, of which the earliest and most important were Sybaris and Croton, founded (according to the usual chronology) in 720 and 708 B.C. The colonisers of Sybaris took advantage of the most extensive area of plain in Calabria, at the eastern side of the more northerly of the two 'waists' of the peninsula, watered by the Crati, Coscile and Ranganello rivers. It resembles a vast and rich theatre-*cavea*, some 20 kilometres broad and 40 deep, and at its furthest point from the sea it leads into a short though by no means easy route across to the Tyrrhenian sea at Belvedere Marittima. The Sybarites lost little time in planting colonies at Laüs (by the mouth of the river Lao) and at Scidrus, the location of which is uncertain, and their wealth and power extended rapidly. The luxury of the city became proverbial, and was paralleled only by that of Siris, which in the mid-sixth century the Sybarites united with Metapontum and Croton to destroy. Towards the end of that century they are said to have dominated four tribes and twenty-five towns, and their territory extended up the Crati valley to Cosenza, from which they had an easy passage to Crotoniate Terina at the mouth of the river Savuto. A bronze plaque recently found at Olympia, the only epigraphic record of Sybaris so far discovered, records their treaty with the Serdaeans, presumably a tribe of this region. Doubtless they also controlled the mountains north of Castrovillari and across the massif of the Sila Grande. Along the coast they had less chance of expansion. Northwards the mountains descend more sharply to the sea, while their neighbours of Croton on the south were constantly at enmity with them. In 511–10 B.C. this hostility culminated in a great battle at the river Traeis (*Trionto*), perhaps the common boundary, after which the victorious Crotoniates, led by their most famous citizen the athlete Milon, destroyed Sybaris utterly. The river

Crati is said to have been diverted so as to flow over the site, and a temple to Athena Crathia was built in the old channel by the Spartan Dorieus, who had arrived at Croton as a timely ally. A remnant of the Sybarites fled to the daughter-cities; some few may have lived on under Crotoniate dominion. But to all intents and purposes the city was erased from the map, and despite much investigation has not as yet been rediscovered. Nor has the search for the refounded Sybaris of 446–5 B.C. and its immediate replacement Thurii (444–3 B.C.), perhaps to be located near Terranova da Sibari, been more successful.

POSIDONIA (PAESTUM)

Of the colonies of Sybaris the most famous and most northerly was that of Posidonia, later and better known as Paestum. Here, early in the seventh century, the Sybarites themselves, or emigrants from Troezen whom they expelled from Sybaris, founded a city in the plain of the Silaris (*Sele*), the limits of which are still marked by a great circuit wall. The area of Paestum is bisected by the modern main road, and the excavated section, on the seaward side of this, contains a large sacred quarter interrupted by the agora and business centre. To the west of the Via Sacra lay a residential district.

Plate 57

Fig. 17

Despite its command of wide agricultural land Posidonia had no strategic advantages and was much exposed to the depredations of the tough Lucanians of the hinterland. Hence its career as an independent Greek city was comparatively brief, and by the end of the fifth century it had been taken over by the Italians. But during its three Greek centuries it attained a prosperity which expressed itself especially in the construction of a remarkable series of temples and shrines. The whole area was particularly distinguished for its cult of Hera, and the countless terracotta dedications from the neighbourhood of the 'Basilica' and the 'Temple of Neptune' (both now shown to be temples of Hera) bear ample witness to the piety of her devotees. Close by, near the mouth of the river, lay the great Heraeum of 'Foce del Sele' with its attendant treasuries, the important sculptures

Plate 63
Plate 64
Plate 62

from which, like the finds from Sestieri's productive excavations in Paestum itself in the early fifties, now enrich the Paestum museum. In the vicinity of the 'Temple of Neptune' Sestieri discovered no fewer than eleven shrines of varying size, all apparently dedicated to Hera. Beyond the agora, the 'Temple of Ceres', notable for unusual details of design and construction, and incorporating an Ionic porch within a Doric peristyle, is now shown to have been dedicated to Athena. Figurine dedications also indicate a thriving Paestan cult of Ilithyia.

Plate 23

CROTON

The site of Croton is not in doubt, and the modern Crotone stands on the headland and uses the port which made its situation defensible and profitable. It gives on to the fertile plain of the Neto, and the coastal lands, interrupted only by low hills around Cutrò, invited expansion. Hence Croton, like the other foundations, gained quick wealth and grew rapidly in population, the city extending on either side of the mouth of the river Esaro. Yet it has almost completely disappeared, and only casual finds in the modern and growing city attest the vanished greatness of its ancient predecessor. Its most famous shrine, that of Hera Lacinia, lay on the Lacinian promontory, to which the single standing column of the fifth-century temple has given its modern name Capo Colonna. This was probably the wealthiest and most frequented sanctuary in southern Italy, and the temple itself was surrounded by a considerable complex of ancillary buildings. But of all the rich offerings nothing remains, and only the temple's terracotta revetments survive in part to give some impression of the quality of the work there.

Crotoniate history in the archaic period was one of ups and downs. The successful wars against Siris and Sybaris have already been mentioned. Between these two high points of success came a disaster in a war against Locri, in which according to the ancient account 15,000 Locrians met and defeated 130,000 Crotoniates by the river Sagra (perhaps the *Allaro*). The victory was so dramatic and complete that divine intervention was called in to explain and enliven the account as handed down. In this period of depression Croton achieved fame of a different kind, as the home of doctors, athletes and philosophers. The ability of Democedes, the court-physician of the Persian king, was such that the best doctors were universally thought, says Herodotus, to come from Croton. Milon, the wrestler who is said to have won thirty-one victories at the great games in Greece, was but the greatest of many Crotoniate champions, for Strabo notes that Croton produced more than any other city. Of Pythagoras and his philosophic school more will be said later. The victory over Sybaris revived Croton's fortunes and left the city as the chief power in southern Italy, but the next generations dissipated this inheritance.

CAULONIA

Of Achaean Caulonia (*Monasterace Marina*), a small settlement of 675–50 B.C. uncomfortably sandwiched between Croton and Locri, little is known. Orsi discovered traces of important and unusual fortifications as well as of a fifth-century Doric temple, which also yielded terracotta decorative work. Caulonia's situation resembled that of Locri; politically it lay within the Crotoniate orbit. Metapontum, also founded from Achaea but a decade or so earlier, lies about fifty kilometres west of Taranto, within whose control it later fell. Its wealth was derived from the wide plain of the Bradano and Busento rivers in the midst of which it lay, and its coins appropriately use an ear of barley as a device. Commerce could travel up the valley of the latter river, across the watershed by Potenza and down to the sea at Paestum, but it is wild territory, and there is little evidence that Metapontine power extended far inland. The sixth century saw Metapontum as a member of the victorious alliance against Siris, and also as rich enough to build the Doric temple of Hera, the remains of which, now known as the Tavole Paladine, are a conspicuous feature of the flat landscape. Of the temple of Apollo Lyceus the terracotta revetments again provide the most impressive relic.

METAPONTUM

Plate 25

TARAS (TARENTUM)

Eastward of this Achaean preserve a colony was planted in 706 B.C., on the traditional dating, by the Spartans. The motives were unusual, for Sparta had no land shortage and her citizens remained uninterested in commerce. The story was that while the flower of Spartan manhood was for long years occupied with the conquest of Messenia, the Spartan women consoled themselves with those who had been left behind, and the resulting offspring were denied full rights of citizenship by the indignant victors on their return. An insurrection was forestalled, and the young malcontents who fled took Delphi's advice and sailed to the west. There, under their leader and *oikistes* Phalanthus, they founded Taras (*Taranto*). There are variant versions of the story, but it is clear that the settlers were called *Parthenioi* (a detail which some of the legend was perhaps created to explain), and that inequality of rights was probably the reason for their migration. Their Laconian origin is assured by the additional witness of their language, place-names, institutions, cults and art.

Phalanthus chose a site the natural advantages of which have made Taranto regain in modern times the importance it won and lost in antiquity. After the decline of the Achaean colonies it remained the most influential of the Greek cities, reaching its peak of prosperity in the fourth century B.C. But in the archaic period it seems to have been comparatively small and unimportant, and rather cut off from the other colonies. Little is known of its early career, and overlaid as it is by a modern city such evidence as has been found has not been systematically recorded. The main harbour (*Marina grande*) is protected from the sea by two islands (*Isole Choirade*), and the entrance to the inner lagoon (*Marina piccola*) is narrowed by the peninsula, now an island, which was the ancient acropolis. Fragments of Doric columns from a temple here have been dated *c.* 575 B.C. But the city spread eastwards, and votive deposits of terracottas indicate a flourishing religious life in the new quarter as early as the seventh century; vases from the cemetery go back to the same period. The government of Taras no doubt owed much to the Spartan model, and in the story of Democedes mention is made of a Tarentine king Aristophilides. Dedications at Delphi record warfare against the Messapians and Peucetians in the early fifth century, and *c.* 473 the Tarentines were overwhelmed by the Iapygians in a slaughter more terrible than anything in Herodotus' experience. The aftermath was a democratic revolution which laid the foundations of Taras' recovery and subsequent expansion.

SIRIS

Of Siris and its short career there is little to be said. Founded by Colophonians who left their native city *c.* 675 B.C. at the time of the Lydian conquest, it stood at the southern end of the Metapontine plain in the neighbourhood of Nova Siri, which preserves its name. At first prosperous, it succumbed *c.* 540 to the triple alliance of Metapontum, Sybaris and Croton. The survivors seem, on the evidence of the coinage, to have removed to Pyxus, a Sybarite colony near Sapri on the Tyrrhenian Sea, which itself did not outlast the fifth century. The territory of Siris was later taken over by the Tarentines, who in 433–2 B.C. planted a colony named Heraclea near Policoro, as a counterpoise to the recently-founded Thurii with which they had disputed its possession.

ELEA (VELIA)

Last of all, Elea (*Velia*). Its foundation *c.* 535 B.C., under the name Hyale, by the Phocaeans expelled from Corsica might perhaps more properly be described in the next section in conjunction with the other Phocaean settlements. A coastal plain hemmed in by the mountains of the Cilento peninsula and watered by the rivers Alento and Fiumarella is interrupted by a narrow ridge running inland at right angles to the sea. On and beside this ridge the Phocaeans built their city, with Rhegine help. The acropolis was well fortified, and while much of the walling now to be seen belongs to the fifth or the fourth century, a polygonal section is presumably contemporary with

Plates 27, 58

E

Elea's foundation. The sanctuaries of the city were strung out along the ridge: most notable among them were the large open precinct of Poseidon, 'the giver of safety', and a fifth-century temple, perhaps of Athena, the substantial remains of which lie beside a mediaeval watch-tower. Here too a section of early masonry, perhaps belonging to the big temple's predecessor, gives us direct contact with the original settlers. Below the acropolis, in a curve of the ridge, lay the agora, and continuing excavation in this area towards the seaward gate will shed more light on the development of the Greek city and of its Roman successor. Isolated as it was, with little territory and at enmity with neighbouring Paestum, Elea managed to remain independent of Lucanian encroachment and looked outwards for prosperity: the Poseidon-cult reflects the Eleans' predominantly maritime interests. But isolation may also breed introspection; that the city quickly produced a flourishing school of philosophy is possibly to be credited in no small measure to the influence which a place may exercise on its people.

Plate 28

Plate 26

Plate 27

THE FARTHEST WEST

Having discovered Sicily and Magna Graecia and the possibilities they offered for colonisation and expansion, the Greeks in general were content to seek no further; and it may be added that the presence of the Etruscans to the north and of the Carthaginians to the west tended to discourage wider search. According to tradition it was the Rhodians who first explored the coasts of the western Mediterranean, founded a settlement in Spain at Rhode, and gave its name, Rhodanus, to the river Rhône. But it was one small city alone which effectively penetrated beyond the accepted limits and carried Hellas permanently into France and Spain. This was Phocaea, on the coast of Asia Minor north of Smyrna, the ultimate ancestor not only of Marseilles, the greatest and most famous of all the Phocaean colonies, but also of Nice, Antibes, Alicante, Malaga and settlements on the Balearic islands. In these cases trade rather than land does seem to have provided the motive, and the Massaliot re-foundation of Rhode even bore the name 'Market' (Emporion, *Ampurias*).

MASSALIA

It is possible that the Phocaeans had developed a trade-route into those waters and had been impressed by the usefulness of permanent bases for contact with the local tribes. There is a romantic story of the founding of Massalia (*Marseilles*), according to which, at the feast when she was to select a husband, the Gallic princess Gyptis passed over her local suitors and chose the Phocaean *oikistes* Protis, who happened just to have arrived. But Thucydides says only that a naval battle had to be fought with the Carthaginians before the colony could be established; and this was an omen for the future. The site for the settlement amply fulfilled expectations. Through it passed goods of Greek manufacture to become the prized possessions of Gallic chieftains, like the magnificent bronze *krater,* made in Laconia or Taras, which awaited the discoverers of the sixth-century royal burial at Vix. The route which it commanded grew accustomed to Greek coinage as a means of exchange, and in a later century the famous *philippeioi,* the gold staters of Philip II of Macedon, were copied and recopied in central Gaul in an increasingly barbarised form. Its influence affected and by degrees hellenised the immediate neighbourhood, marking it off from the less civilised north, so that at a later stage, when the Romans took it over, it was an already-settled *provincia,* a name which as Provence it has kept ever since. But to the west as well as to the east of the Rhône discoveries of Greek material in Gallic *oppida,* of which Ensérune in Hérault is perhaps the best example, emphasise the growing extent of Massaliot power.

Plates 31–33

Plate 29

MASSALIOT EXPANSION

After a promising beginning Massaliot trade with the interior seems to have been checked, perhaps because of the movements which replaced the Hallstatt by the La Tène I culture, and the fifth century was, for Massalia, one of depression. In the fourth and third centuries, however, the Massaliots expanded their territory by establishing outposts at Theline near Arles, Glanum near St Rémy, and elsewhere. But their efforts here were consequent upon the failure of their earlier coastal enterprises in southern Spain, where Carthaginian encroachment gradually overcame the Phocaean foundations and isolated the Greeks in the Gulf of Lyons. Ampurias, which has been particularly well studied, remained the farthest outpost of Greek influence and survived to become a focal point for the Roman penetration of Spain in the third century.

Despite its wealth and importance, or perhaps in a sense because of them, ancient Massalia has left only a poor legacy to modern Marseilles, which used to be decribed as 'la cité antique sans antiquité'. Wartime destruction in the area of the Vieux Port, the ancient Lacydon, revealed part of a Greek theatre, and the pottery so well attested in the surrounding country is now well evidenced in the metropolis itself.

Plate 30

ALALIA

Carthage and Etruria, alike threatened by Greek activity in the west, combined to resist it. The Phocaeans had attempted to settle Alalia, on the east coast of Corsica, *c.* 560 B.C., as a useful way-station on the westward route, but some twenty-five years later they were attacked by an allied Etrusco-Punic fleet and though victorious they realised that the site was too insecure for a permanent colony. After some adventures they established themselves at Elea, within the Greek 'area of settlement'. With the loss of Spain to Carthage, the Western Greeks were in general on the defensive by the end of the sixth century. In the fifth they had to face both Carthaginian and Etruscan attacks on their main positions, and their enterprise in the farthest west was never again what it had been in the earliest days.

DATES IN EARLY GREEK HISTORY

One of the most difficult problems in early Greek history—perhaps the most difficult problem of all—is that of fitting our defective information into a satisfactory framework of chronology. No dates can be regarded as fixed and acceptable unless they are backed by clear and agreed literary testimony or by archaeological correlation with a chronology assured by a well-established external system, for example with Egyptian parallels. Since, for the Greeks, contemporary historical writing did not begin until the fifth century, earlier data preserved in the literature are for the most part traditional and offer few secure points before 500 B.C.

Without firm 'pegs' provided by fixed, or 'absolute', dates on which to hang a chronological sequence, archaeology can suggest a chronology no more than relative, based for example on differences in character detected in a series of discovered objects, as between a supposed 'earlier' and 'later' type, on the difference in the level at which objects on a given site are found, and on the comparison of objects associated in the same grave or stratum, with the assistance of similar objects found elsewhere. Such comparative methods, based principally on the development of Greek pottery, have produced a workable system of relative chronology, and the interlocking of its components has made it, with time, almost self-supporting. Within limits it can be known how long a certain style of pottery lasted and, as a result, what is the date of an occupation-level at which it is found or of a tomb among whose furniture it figures. But even with a margin of error of two or three decades it is desirable to be able to express such a chronology in terms of years B.C. rather than in terms of an artistic style or a more generalised era. For instance, since the Athenian acropolis is known to have been sacked by the Persians in 480 B.C., it can at least be said of the material found in the destruction-fill that it antedates the

Persian War. But on a comparative basis this material covers a long span, and to relate it and other archaic material to a serviceable time-scale further fixed points are required. It is not the least service of the Western Greeks that they have, indirectly, provided this, and it is to them that the expression of archaic Greek chronology in a fairly firm sequence with a year-by-year dating is mainly owed.

THUCYDIDES' FOUNDATION-DATES

This chronology is based on Thucydides' account of earlier Sicilian history in Book VI, with which he introduces his narrative of the Athenian expedition against Syracuse. There he gives details of the foundation of many of the colonies, and good use has already been made of it in this chapter. He provides two distinct sequences, with relative dates. In the one he refers to the settlement of Syracuse in relation to that of Naxos, and to the settlements of Leontini, Catana, Megara (with Selinus) and Gela (with Acragas) in relation to Syracuse; in the other he relates the foundations of the Syracusan colonies to Syracuse herself. Thucydides' date for the foundation of Syracuse is thus fundamental to a chronology which, by giving a series of starting dates for various sites, enables the earliest pottery found in them to be fitted into a firm system. That this date is 734 or 733 B.C. is to be inferred from other early evidence. To these data may be added the fixed point of the destruction of Megara (483–2 B.C.).

An alternative series of dates was provided by Eusebius, the bishop-historian of Caesarea (third century A.D.), and he also deals with the Italian colonies, with which Thucydides was not concerned. It is probable that the variants reflect faulty transmission of a generally accepted scheme, and it seems likely that the tradition of the *order* in which the colonies were founded has a sound basis, possibly in the work of Antiochus of Syracuse. It is an order with which archaeological discoveries appear to be in general agreement. As to dating, however, particular difficulties have arisen over Selinus. Here it was originally thought that the

CHRONOLOGY OF SELINUS

earliest pottery (Early Corinthian) corroborated the Thucydidean date of 628 B.C., but more recently the discovery of Late Protocorinthian pottery has suggested that an earlier date is to be preferred. This would fit with the 650 B.C. to be derived from Eusebius (651 in Diodorus, who dates the foundation of Selinus 242 years before its destruction in 409). To lower the date of Protocorinthian pottery by a quarter of a century is too drastic a remedy, simple though it seems, for the dating of the Corinthian series, elaborated by Johansen and Payne with minor subsequent modifications, is cardinal to the whole complex structure of relative chronology, and the effect of such a change would be an undue compression of all subsequent development down to the end of the sixth century. Thucydides may have been mistaken in the date he gives for Selinus, but this supposition in turn leaves his other dates open to suspicion and they too are cardinal to the chronological pattern. A hopeful thesis that Selinus was founded twice, Thucydides taking account only of the second and more important foundation, is hardly convincing.

It is at least clear that the dates which have been quoted are in the right region. The early colonies, with the exceptions of Ischia and Cumae, belong roughly to the last third of the eighth century, and any dating system that is evolved for them ought to be allowed a fairly generous degree of flexibility. The overlap of pottery-styles, the time to be assumed between the dates of a city's foundation and its first grave-group, the extent to which pre-colonisation imports may be admitted—all may play a part in affecting the archaeological contribution to this particular study. But because of Thucydides' intervention the rôle of the western Greeks has become of supreme importance to the whole chronological problem of archaic Greece, and they may earn the historian's extra respect on that account.

CHAPTER IV

The Story of the Western Greeks

SICILY IN THE SIXTH CENTURY

BY THE BEGINNING of the sixth century the Greek settlements had taken root and prospered. Although, as has been described, the Greeks did not embark on historical writing until the fifth century, tradition for the preceding two or three generations was well-founded and generally coherent, being reinforced by the literature of the time, particularly that of the lyric poets, and by local records. Much valuable material, derived from oral and written sources, was collected in the later fifth century by the Syracusan Antiochus, and since he no doubt lies behind a good deal of what later authors say of Sicilian affairs in this period it may be accepted that the account to be derived from them is sound enough in its general lines. Archaeology and a growing literary record can thus combine to bring Greek Sicily out of the mists of its earliest years and to make possible a connected if at times bald narrative of what happened.

GREEKS AND CARTHAGINIANS

Two particular features of Sicilian development in this century deserve to be stressed, and both were to be repeated in the century following. One of these, the crystallisation of enmity between the Greeks and Carthaginians, arose from the check which Carthage now made to further Greek expansion. What happened in Gaul and Spain has already been described. In Sicily, where the Phoenicians may not have been established much before the Greeks, no opposition had been offered to the settlement of Selinus and Himera. But when, at about the time of the foundation of Acragas, a contingent of Rhodians and Cnidians under Pentathlus attempted to colonise Lilybaeum (*Marsala*), near Phoenician Motya, and assisted Selinus in a war against Segesta, the Phoenicians joined the Elymians in defeating the allies, in killing Pentathlus, and in extinguishing the new colony. The surviving Cnidians sailed off to found a settlement in the Lipari islands from which they could prey on merchantmen and challenge the Etruscan domination of the seas, so marked after Alalia. The Selinuntines probably came to terms with Carthage: the insecurity of their position made it desirable, their evident prosperity makes it likely. The Phoenician danger, demanding resolute defence, also may have prompted the Acragantines to accept the tyranny of Phalaris and to raise their strong fortifications. Himera, equally threatened, put itself under the same protection.

Warfare with Carthage continued. A Carthaginian general Malchus apparently had considerable success, but his energies were later diverted to Sardinia. This island, to judge from a number of scattered references, the Greeks greatly coveted; but they never acquired it. Its conquest by Carthage, paralleled by Etruscan control of Corsica, further hemmed them into their area of settlement. Etruscan and Carthaginian fleets controlled the seas, and Etruscan pressure by land on the Italian colonies was halted only by a desperate Cumaean victory. Even so, Cumae found it advisable to follow a conciliatory policy towards the Etruscans, and gave refuge to Tarquinius Superbus on his expulsion from Rome. Etruscan influence was at its most pronounced in Campania at this period—not only politically. It has for instance left its mark on the sixth-century Doric temple in the Foro Triangolare at Pompeii.

Plate 35

EXPEDITION OF DORIEUS

A final attempt to win western Sicily for the Greeks was made by Dorieus, half-brother of King Cleomenes of Sparta. Baffled of the throne which Herodotus' informants implied was rightfully his, he set out *c.* 514 B.C. to found a colony in Libya; when this failed he tried again, this time at Sicilian Eryx (*Erice*), in the very heart of the Phoenician zone, where his colony was apparently named Heraclea. But he and his colleagues were

Plate 36

killed by the Carthaginians and Elymians, who once more combined to resist Greek penetration. One of his lieutenants, Euryleon, seized Heraclea Minoa and later Selinus, where he dispossessed a tyrant Peithagoras, perhaps by provoking a reaction to the latter's pro-Punic policy. But Euryleon was assassinated, Selinus reverted to her friendship with Carthage, and the Acragantines took the opportunity to seize Minoa and strengthen their boundaries.

It is worth noticing, perhaps, that the resistance of the Carthaginians and Elymians to Greek political penetration in no way interrupted the cultural influences which the Greek colonists were able to exert. The Hellenism of Segesta has already been mentioned, and Hellenic elements in Siculo-Punic art become marked. Inscriptions from Motya suggest that it contained a fair proportion of Greek or Greek-speaking inhabitants. Nevertheless, at the end of the century it seemed likely that a decision as between Greek and Carthaginian in Sicily would have to be fought out on a grand scale. When the moment came, the Greeks were fortunate in having a leader of the necessary calibre.

THE SICILIAN TYRANNIES

The second feature of Sicilian sixth-century history is in fact the emergence of this very element of autocratic leadership, the extra-constitutional 'tyrant'. Tyrants were endemic in Sicily throughout its independence, and no land, wrote the historian Justin, was more prolific in them. Though tyrannies existed in a number of cities of Aegean Greece during the seventh and sixth centuries, the tyrants in Sicily seem to have been especially remarkable in the extent of their power and in the bloodthirsty and callous severity with which they exercised it. By the fifth and fourth centuries Aegean Greece had well learned some bitter lessons, and coups d'état which might institute a personal dictatorship were generally avoided, so that tyrannies there are less in evidence. But in the west they continued to flourish with great success and ferocity, and provided all Hellas with examples to admire and fear. All the same, there can be no doubt that the tyrants provided the Sicilians, though at a cost, with the unity they needed. Stress is sometimes laid on their cruelty and other shortcomings to the detriment of the very real contribution they made to the Greek achievement.

The first Sicilian city to fall under such a despotism seems to have been Leontini, where one Panaetius seized power *c.* 610 B.C. His method, repeated on numerous occasions by later imitators, was that of gaining popularity as a military commander and championing the under-privileged against the ruling oligarchy. Phalaris was more famous and more cruel. The Selinuntine tyrants—for Peithagoras was one of a series—were probably more pacific. Like all such despots the tyrants expressed themselves in great architectural works, and the wealth of surviving monuments of the archaic period is attributable not only to the general prosperity of the time but also in some degree to the prevalence of autocrats with thoughts of advertisement and national prestige.

HIPPOCRATES OF GELA

The great succession of tyrants begins *c.* 505 B.C. with the establishment of a tyranny in Gela by Cleander, a wealthy Geloan who overthrew the existing oligarchy. On his assassination he was succeeded by his brother Hippocrates, whose vigorous and ruthless activities made him within seven years master of all eastern Sicily. He seems to have been boundlessly ambitious and completely without principle, and he tried to extend his dominion over Greek and Sicel alike. The brutality of his conquests and the cynicism of his dealings with cities and individuals set a grisly pattern for his no less ambitious successors.

Herodotus mentions his conquest of Callipolis, Naxos, Zancle and Leontini. Zancle he tried to retain by double-crossing his own lieutenant Scythes, sub-tyrant there in his interest, taking the part of a Samian contingent who seized the city during Scythes' absence with the support of Anaxilas, tyrant of Rhegium. But Anaxilas as a good Rhegine had an interest in the ownership of Zancle, where in the event he put more settlers, partly to watch the Samians' doubtful loyalties—in the process renaming the city Messana, Messenians being prominent among the new colonists.

Earlier in the sequence of Hippocrates' successes must have come the subjugation of the Sicels of the Geloan hinterland. His crowning achievement was a successful war against Syracuse. Approaching from the south he first destroyed Camarina, which had revived after its defeat by the Syracusans, and then he defeated the Syracusans themselves at the river Helorus. But a siege of Syracuse was a formidable operation, and he allowed himself to be persuaded by Corinthian and Corcyarean mediators into withdrawing after accepting Camarina and its territory as ransom for his Syracusan prisoners. He was killed *c.* 490 while on campaign against the Sicels of Hybla, leaving his two young sons to the guardianship of his lieutenant Gelon, son of Deinomenes. The Geloans rebelled against the tyranny, but were quelled by Gelon, who was apparently more popular than his former chief and his family. The boys were set aside, and Gelon took over supreme power.

GELON BECOMES TYRANT

External adventure being the surest safeguard against internal insecurity, Gelon's programme is said to have included a war to avenge the death of Dorieus and a design on the coast of Africa. Since Hippocrates had created a navy, this was by no means an impossible scheme. But it brought on, under his autocratic control, the decisive clash with Carthage, and to this, as we have seen, the strands of archaic Sicilian development all led.

THE RISE OF SYRACUSE

We know little about the early part of Gelon's tyranny. He installed a sub-tyrant named Glaucus in Camarina, and we next find him called in to help the Gamoroi, the Syracusan aristocrats, who had been expelled in a democratic revolution and had taken refuge at Casmenae. Tyrants were normally no friends of oligarchs, but Gelon seized the opportunity to get possession of Syracuse without opposition. This coup was the fulfilment of Hippocrates' ambitions, and Gelon carried the logic of it a stage further by leaving Gela under his brother Hieron and transferring his capital to Syracuse. To enlarge and strengthen the city he removed to it the entire populations of Camarina and Megara Hyblaea and many of the Geloans also, added fortifications, and began to build a grand fleet. Envoys from the Greeks, seeking allies against Persia, were promised 200 hundred ships and 20,000 hoplites, provided that Gelon was made supreme commander—an offer which they rejected with some disgust.

THERON OF ACRAGAS

The only city large enough to oppose this Syracusan empire was Acragas, and here there now reigned a more peaceable but no less splendid tyrant, Theron, of the aristocratic family of the Emmenidae. Gelon possibly sought his alliance soon after he became tyrant (488 B.C.), for the purposes of his projected Carthaginian war, and this was cemented by Gelon's marriage to Theron's daughter Demarete and that of Theron with Gelon's niece. The two chief cities thus found it possible to co-exist, and it was as well that they did, for the Carthaginians, perhaps already provoked, were now prepared to descend on Sicily in force.

GELON'S WAR WITH CARTHAGE

Anaxilas of Rhegium, who had maintained his hold on Messana, had made an alliance, confirmed by marriages, with Terillus tyrant of Himera, himself an ally of Carthage. The Carthaginians were for these two, as for Selinus, the only bulwark against the Syracuse-Acragas axis, and when *c.* 483 B.C. Theron resuscitated the old policy of Phalaris by expelling Terillus and uniting Himera and Acragas under a single anti-Carthaginian control, it was natural for Terillus to appeal to them. Their preparations took three years and the expedition was formidable, though modern opinion finds Herodotus' figure of 300,000 for the army which crossed to Panormus too much to accept. Gelon and Theron are said to have put 50,000 men into the field: it may be that both sides were fairly evenly matched. The Carthaginians, commanded by Hamilcar, grandson of that Malchus who had in his day won successes against the Greeks, marched to Himera and laid siege to it. Gelon, whose forces were mobilised and in readiness, took immediate action. The details of the ensuing battle remain obscure, though both Herodotus and Diodorus have lively (and differing) accounts. It is said to have taken place on the same day as the battle of Salamis (or Thermopylae), and the Greek victory was overwhelming. Hamilcar was killed, those of his ships which were not burned were wrecked, an immense number of Carthaginians were killed or captured, and, adds Diodorus, 'only a few survivors in one small boat reached home to give the brief news that all who had crossed over to Sicily had perished.'

Gelon and Theron did not follow up this victory by carrying the war to Africa or even attacking the Carthaginian cities in Sicily. They were content to make peace and to confirm their hold on the Greek area by accepting the alliance of the cities which had opposed them. In celebration of his triumph Gelon issued commemorative ten-drachma pieces which, since they are said to have been minted from a gift made by Carthage to Gelon's wife, were known as Demareteia. A temple was built at Himera from the spoils, and in Syracuse itself the archaic shrine of Athena was replaced by a new Doric temple, now incorporated in the Cathedral. Theron for his part began the temple of Olympian Zeus, one of the largest as well as one of the most unusual of all Greek temples: it was never finished and its details remain uncertain, but it had no peristyle, half-columns were engaged in the outer walls, and a series of colossal

Plate 42*a*
Plate 34
Plate 39
Plate 18
Fig. 8

figures with arms behind their heads were incorporated in it, bearing perhaps like Atlas the burden of some part of the superstructure.

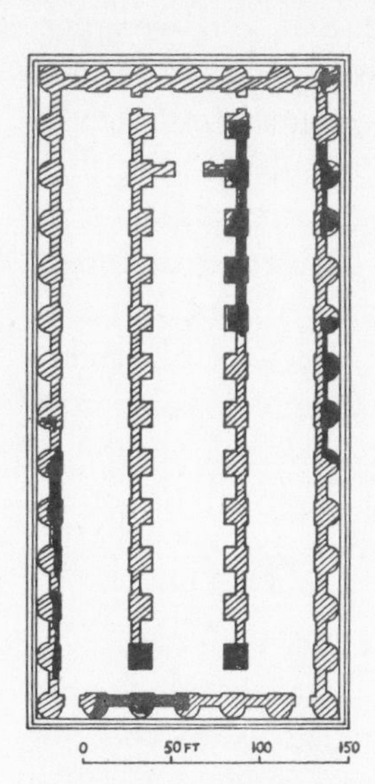

Fig. 8. Temple of Zeus Olympius at Acragas: ground plan

HIERON OF SYRACUSE

Neither tyrant long survived his moment of glory. Gelon died in 478 and was succeeded by Hieron, who installed a younger brother Polyzelus in Gela. The two subsequently quarrelled, and Polyzelus sought the help of Theron, his father-in-law, but conflict was avoided thanks to the intervention of the poet Simonides; thereafter Polyzelus, whose vicissitudes are reflected in the altered inscription on the base of his dedication at Delphi, the 'Delphic Charioteer', drops out of history. Hieron carried forward his brother's policy of strengthening Syracusan control by removal of populations, settling in Leontini the people of Naxos and Catana, while to Catana, renamed Aetna, he sent fresh settlers. But his greatest exploit, which again (as Pindar took care to note) paralleled Gelon's achievement, was the naval battle in which as the ally of Cumae he defeated the Etruscan fleet (474 B.C.). The danger from the north was checked and, unlike that from the west, did not revive. A helmet inscribed as a dedication of spoil from this battle and found at Olympia was presented by George IV to the British Museum.

Plate 38

Hieron died in 466, six years after Theron, and in neither Syracuse nor Acragas did the tyranny last long, although in the former at least it took stiff fighting to drive out Thrasybulus, the youngest of Gelon's brothers. In both cities democracies replaced the autocracies, and in both, too, there was difficulty in disposing of the large number of mercenaries and foreigners whom the tyrants had kept there for their support. In the end many of these were settled in Messana, now freed from dependence on Rhegium; other cities were repopulated with their previous inhabitants, among them Catana, which also reverted to its own name, that of Aetna being transferred to Inessa, whither the Aetnaeans were themselves removed. But these new Sicilian democracies were unstable, and excess of liberty became as fatal as excess of oppression. The large population of Syracuse in particular was a prey to the emotional appeal of the demagogue or the military hero, and the instability of the Syracusan *demos* is in contrast with the solid and efficient system of the Athenians. Although Plato rejected the folly of the Athenian democracy which had, in his view, murdered his teacher Socrates, it was the democracy of Syracuse which gave him and Aristotle the example of that mingled apathy and rash emotionalism on which an ambitious tyrant could batten. The supreme western example helped to make democracy, for them, the worst-but-one of all modes of government.

ART AND SOCIETY UNDER THE TYRANTS

Although the tyrants' politics were ruthless and oppressive, sparing neither city nor individual in pursuit of their ambitions, they saved the Greek West from the dangers which had threatened it and, at a price, gave it unity and power. The brilliance of their achievements was reflected in that of their courts. The victories of the Emmenid and Deinomenid families in the Greek games were sung by Pindar; Bacchylides and Simonides, Epicharmus and Aeschylus found encouragement at Hieron's court, and the tyrant built a new theatre, the trapezoidal plan of which is still visible despite later remodelling, for the better presentation of the newly developed drama. Theron's temple of Olympian Zeus has already been discussed, and the temple of Athena underlying the church of S. Maria dei Greci is his also. He is known also to have improved the fortifications and water-supply of the city, and he enjoyed a popularity which Hieron

Plate 37

Plate 41

Fig. 8

never achieved. It would, however, be unjustified to regard these building-programmes and the encouragement of literature and the arts as exclusively the prerogative of the tyrants. Democracies did not enter chariots at Olympia and engage the lyric poets to eulogise their victories, but that building continued unabated is clear from the temples of 'Juno' and 'Concord' at Acragas, both of which are later in date than the expulsion of Theron's son Thrasydaeus; and the continuance of an assured welcome to the leading literary figures of Greece is suggested by Aeschylus' presence in Gela, where he died in 456 B.C. (it is said by a blow from a tortoise-shell dropped on his bald head by an eagle who mistook it for a rock).

Plate 17

Fig. 9

Fig. 9. Gem, formerly in the Stosch collection, depicting the death of Aeschylus: size of original (now apparently lost) not stated

SYRACUSE MAINTAINS ITS LEADERSHIP

The island continued to be as turbulent under the popular governments as it had been under the tyrants, and the hegemony of Syracuse was maintained, notwithstanding the change of régime. The Syracusans were again powerful enough to check the Etruscans, and in two expeditions in 453–2 B.C. they seized Elba and invaded Corsica. Suspicious of their ambitions, other cities sought allies where they could. In the mid-450's Leontini and Rhegium made alliances with Athens, as did Segesta, lately perhaps the loser in a war with Selinus. The sympathies of Syracuse and her satellites were more naturally with the Peloponnesians. There seems to have been a flourishing export trade in corn to the Peloponnese, against which the Athenians had to take action when war broke out, and in 431 B.C. the Spartans felt able to call on their allies in the west for quotas of money and ships, although neither, as it seems, was forthcoming.

Within Syracuse itself the democrats were nervous about the possibility of a revived tyranny. 'Petalism', a system derived from and similar to the Athenian ostracism, was designed to get rid of would-be tyrants whether real or imagined. But the greatest danger to the Syracusans, and indeed to the Sicilian Greeks as a whole, lay in the career of Ducetius, a Sicel leader with the ability to unify his people and to weld them into a formidable power.

DUCETIUS AND THE SICELS

Ducetius had brought Sicel help to Syracuse when the tyranny was overthrown. Some six years later he established himself at Menaenum (*Mineo*), a mountain stronghold near Caltagirone, and is spoken of by Diodorus, the sole authority for his career, as king of the Sicels. From here he won over or subdued nearly all the Sicel settlements, and became strong enough to move into the plain and found a new capital at Palice. He then turned his attention to the Greeks and captured Aetna, formerly the Sicel Inessa; subsequent action in the territory of Acragas led to a battle in which he defeated an allied Syracusan-Acragantine force. There is a dedication at Olympia which may represent Sicel gratitude for this triumph. But in the next year the tables were turned and the danger averted. Ducetius after his defeat took the risk of riding alone to Syracuse and appearing as a suppliant at the altar in the agora. The Syracusans to their credit respected his sanctuary and sent him to

Corinth, where he lived in retirement for five years. In 446 he reappeared as founder of a new city, Kale Akte, east of Cefalù, not perhaps without Syracusan support. At least, so the Acragantines thought, and warfare ensued between Syracuse and Acragas in which the latter was defeated. Ducetius died in 440, and with him all hope of a strong Sicel power in the interior of the island: but it took one more Syracusan-Sicel war (439) before the Greeks could regard the situation as satisfactory.

ATHENS' FIRST SICILIAN EXPEDITION

In 433 B.C., when the war with Sparta was clearly approaching, the Athenians reaffirmed their alliances with Rhegium and Leontini, and added to the record of their treaty with Segesta a similar treaty with another Elymian town, Halicyae. But the Western Greeks remained aloof from the conflict, exercising a benevolent neutrality towards their friends. By 427, however, war had broken out between Leontini and Syracuse, neighbours too close to remain indifferent to each other. The Leontines sent the orator Gorgias at the head of an embassy seeking the help of their Athenian allies, and the Athenians, despite commitments elsewhere, allowed themselves to be persuaded. They no doubt felt that the Sicilians, if busy fighting each other, would be less able to support the Peloponnesians, and the size of the fleet they sent, twenty ships under Laches and Charoeades, indicates their wish to keep the pot boiling. More cities, in Italy as well as Sicily, became involved and operations, mainly centring on the straits of Messina, were desultory and inconclusive. The allies demanded more positive help, and the Athenians grew to realise that Sicily offered possibilities. Hence in 425 a fleet of forty ships was sent—an advance party under Pythodorus taking over from Laches early in the year. This larger expedition made a promising start: Naxos and Rhegium were successfully defended against forces from Messana and Locri, allies of Syracuse. But the Syracusans, now less well placed to win the war, encouraged a movement towards peace begun by a separate armistice between Gela and Camarina.

Making a parade of closing Sicilian ranks against external imperialism, they sent to a peace conference convened in Gela their leading statesman Hermocrates, a man whom Thucydides saw as a Sicilian Pericles, and into whose mouth he puts a sharp exposé of Athenian policy in Sicily. Peace was made, and Pythodorus and his two colleagues had to return to Athens, there to stand trial for having taken bribes. The people, perhaps overestimating what they had achieved and what it was possible to achieve, could not credit that they could otherwise have allowed their grasp of Sicilian affairs to be so supinely relaxed.

ATHENS' GREAT SICILIAN EXPEDITION

The Athenians did not forget a prospect which had by now captured their imaginations. Sicily was wealthy, and riven as it was with inter-city jealousies it offered scope for enterprise and ambition. In 422 they sent Phaeax on a goodwill mission to lay the foundations of an anti-Syracusan alliance, but it was not until 415 that, freed of their other undertakings, they had the men and money to launch their great and fatal expedition against Syracuse. With its origin in an appeal for help by Segesta against Selinus, it developed into a plan to subjugate all Sicily and principally the key to Sicily, Syracuse. The story, to which Thucydides devoted his sixth and seventh books, has deservedly remained one of literature's most tragic masterpieces. No paraphrase can do it justice, and no attempt at one will be made here. It would serve only to spoil the impact of an account which awaits the reader who has yet to come to it as an enviable literary experience. We have Plutarch's word that Philistus, the contemporary Syracusan historian, rose to equal heights. Timaeus, who re-worked the story more than a century later, spoiled it by exaggerated rhetorical effect and missed the impressive simplicity of the fifth-century writers.

THE ATHENIAN DISASTER

The Athenians lost, totally, two great fleets, and handicapped themselves thenceforward in their war against Sparta, even though their failure in Sicily was not the direct cause of their final defeat in the Aegean. Of the proud armament, 134 warships and 27,000 men, that sailed in June 415, and of the 73 ships and 15,000 men who tried to salvage the enterprise in 413, little remained; 7,000 survivors were imprisoned in the quarries of Syracuse, where disease took further toll. Of those who were sold into slavery some escaped and so reached home, while a few earned freedom by their ability to quote Euripides for their culture-hungry masters. The tragedy and the completeness of the Athenian disaster are enhanced by Athens' nearness to success. As Nicias and Demosthenes led their broken troops south to their final ruin beside the river Assinarus, in a desperate attempt to escape, they could reflect that there had indeed been a moment when the Syracusans had been on the point of surrender. The Athenians in fact had chances to achieve their ambitions, both at the beginning and in the course of the siege, but accident or ignorance of the possibilities prevented them. Although Nicias may be censured for superstition and irresolution, the project was not beyond Athens' means, nor were the forces or generals inadequate. The recall of the flamboyant Alcibiades was not a decisive factor, and the reasons for failure advanced by Thucydides are not borne out by his own narrative. Errors were made on both sides, but Syracuse had fortune for an ally, and in Hermocrates and the Spartan Gylippus found leaders to sustain morale and take advantage of the enemy's mistakes. The Syracusans celebrated their deliverance with an issue of ten-drachma pieces in imitation of the Demareteia, a numismatic triumph worthy of the occasion.

Plate 42*b*

ITALY IN THE FIFTH CENTURY

Scanty though our information is about the Sicilian Greeks in the fifth century, concerning their compatriots in Italy we are in far worse condition. Rhegium and Locri were near enough to Sicily to be involved in Sicilian animosities, and Rhegine enmity with Syracuse as well as Locri meant that the Locrians remained firm Syracusan allies. The tyranny of Anaxilas passed at his death (476) to his two sons under the guardianship of

Micythus, whose ten-year regency was conducted with remarkable honesty. One of his dedications at Olympia, which Herodotus says were numerous, still survives. In 461 the tyranny gave place to a democracy. The Rhegines had been Tarentine allies in the fatal battle with the Iapygians. After 444 Taras was also menaced by Thurii, where the new settlers looked for local support. They became allies of the Messapians, and an inscribed bronze *caduceus* seems to be evidence of an alliance with the Brundisians. But Taras managed to claim and settle the

Fig. 10

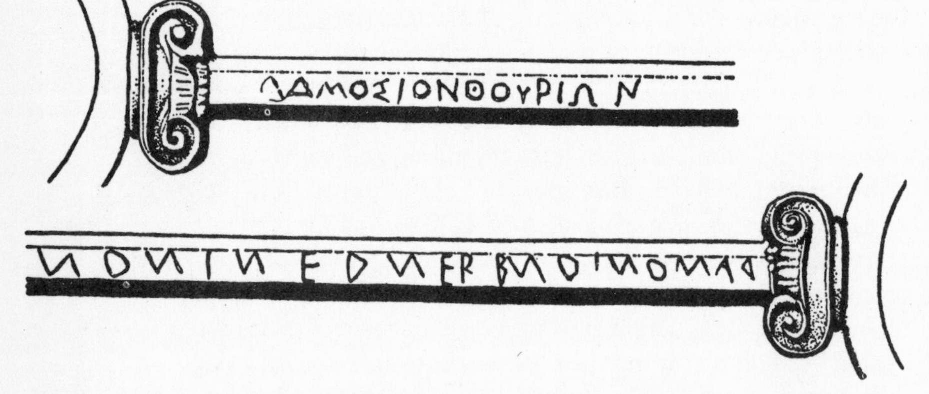

Fig. 10. Bronze 'caduceus' commemorating the treaty between Thurii and Brundisium, c. 440 B.C., now at Venice in a private collection: drawing based on C. De Simone, Archaeologia Classica, *VIII, 1956, figs. 1–2*

territory of Siris and to absorb Metapontum, and a spear-butt dedicated at Olympia testifies to Tarentine gratitude for a victory over the Thurians.

PYTHAGORAS AT CROTON

While Taras, despite early setbacks, increased in power, the Crotoniates declined from the peak of success they had attained on the destruction of Sybaris. Croton was under the general leadership of the followers of the philosopher Pythagoras, whose teaching advocated, like that of Gandhi in our time, a 'way of life' with political consequences. The influence of the Pythagorean clubs, though obscure to us, was clearly very real and widespread among the Italian cities and turned at least the Crotoniate government into an aristocracy of a philosophic *élite*. But a reaction drove Pythagoras to Metapontum, where he died, and according to Polybius' account the destruction of the Pythagorean domination eventually caused great bloodshed and upheaval. Of a war in which Croton suffered at the hands of Locri, Hipponium and Medma, part of a bronze shield found at Olympia gives a hitherto unsuspected glimpse.

The Italian cities achieved some unity in the hostility, open or veiled, with which they greeted the Athenians' great expedition against Syracuse. Even the Rhegines found their loyalty strained, and after the *débâcle* the Thurians, Locrians and Tarentines joined Syracuse in prosecuting the war in the Aegean. Meanwhile the fifth-century temples in the various cities attest a flourishing religious life and an economic prosperity to enhance it. Locri, Croton, Hipponium, Taras, Posidonia and Elea can all show sanctuaries built or rebuilt in this period. Yet the pressure of the Italians of the interior made their prosperity precarious, and towards the end of the century Cumae, Posidonia and Pyxus at least appear to have succumbed to it.

Plates 20, 26, 64

DIONYSIUS I OF SYRACUSE

From this point to their final conquest by Rome, the history of the Greeks in the west is dominated by Syracuse, and Syracuse in her turn is dominated by a series of individuals—tyrants, kings and 'liberators'—around whom her story revolves. This is not a mere accident of historical writing, for example because biographies of the liberators Dion and Timoleon are extant among Plutarch's *Lives*. It was clearly the pattern of Sicilian development, reflected for the fourth century in the histories of the Sicilians Philistus and Timaeus and of the eastern Greeks Ephorus and Theopompus, from whom, *via* Diodorus, it comes down to us. Philistus and Timaeus were both strongly partisan, the one a friend and the other a bitter enemy of the Syracusan tyranny. Timaeus, the more flamboyant, was the more popular and may have impressed his viewpoint the more effectively upon the tradition; Philistus resembled Thucydides in style and technique and was less to the taste of a later generation.

This was a century in which the brilliant individual came more and more to impose himself on the structure of the Greek *polis.* A society which had rejected the archaic tyrannies began to return, in theory and practice, to the monarchic idea as a solution to the Greeks' endemic political discord, while leaders arose who by force of arms or personality were able to reach a position of command. In the east Philip and Alexander of Macedon brought to an end the Greece of independent city-states, which henceforward lived in the shadow of the Hellenistic kings. But it was in the west that the pattern of successful monarchy in the *polis*-world was first sketched out, and where an imposed solution to the problem of Greek disunity created a city-state empire second in extent only to Athens' fifth-century League, though in form and character very different from it.

SYRACUSE AFTER THE ATHENIAN DEFEAT

For Thucydides one of the great features of the struggle between Athens and Syracuse, which made it radically different from that between Athens and Sparta, was that both cities were democracies, on the crest of the same wave, with the same principles and the same dynamism. But, as has already been mentioned, the Syracusans lacked Athenian moderation and judgement in working the democratic system, and showed themselves, even when they achieved liberty, undeserving of it. The immediate consequences of their victory over Athens foreshadow what was to come. Hermocrates took an expedition to the Aegean to prosecute the war with the Athenians. In his absence his more extreme opponents obtained power, exiled him, and entered on a war with Carthage which was to prove their undoing. The Carthaginians, called in by Segesta against Selinus, made energetic preparations and with 100,000 men under Hannibal, grandson of that Hamilcar defeated seventy years earlier, captured and sacked Selinus (409–8), a success immediately followed by the destruction of Himera. There, to appease Hamilcar's shade, 3,000 prisoners were piously tortured and killed. The sudden return of Hermocrates provoked more disorder among the already disordered Syracusans, but although he and most of his followers were killed the democrats lost their grip on affairs by their mismanagement of the defence of Acragas (406–5), which was abandoned to Carthage.

DIONYSIUS SEIZES POWER

In spring 405 Hermocrates' ambitious lieutenant, the twenty-three-year-old Dionysius, one of the few to have escaped the slaughter of Hermocrates' party, took advantage of popular reaction to be nominated supreme commander. He was voted a bodyguard, and controlled thenceforward by force or fraud the destinies and persons of the Syracusans. A man without pity or principle, efficient in the preservation of his despotism, he reigned for thirty-eight years. During this time, while enhancing the material prosperity of Syracuse and creating a unified Western Greek world under Syracusan control, he did much to destroy the true character of the Greek settlements by his ruthless removal or enslavement of those opposed to him; and by his introduction of aliens subservient to himself into the citizen bodies of Syracuse and its dependent cities he diluted the Hellenic element there and created serious difficulties for the future.

It might be unjust to Dionysius to suggest that his rule was unpopular in Syracuse. When a tyranny is overthrown its erstwhile supporters tend to rival one another in vilifying it, and the tradition that Dionysius executed more than 10,000 citizens probably derives from such a source, which Timaeus would have used with relish. Certainly preservation of Dionysius' power was, for Dionysius, the most important object of policy, and to it he was prepared to sacrifice the interests of Syracuse and of Hellenism. The threat of Carthage was useful to him in this connexion, and although in his first Carthaginian war (397–2) he may have aimed to expel the Carthaginians from Sicily altogether, the wisdom of his riper years gave the second and third wars (387–78 and 368–7) a more limited scope. He can be credited as little with Panhellenism as with any other sentiment. To guard against any Syracusan discontent, he converted Ortygia into a palace-stronghold garrisoned with 10,000 mercenaries. Offices and commands were retained within his family and circle of friends, but none of these could feel himself safe from the despot's wrath if he appeared to deserve it.

DIONYSIUS AMBITIONS

Dionysius was thus a tyrant in the grand manner. All his actions—his defeats as well as his victories—have a new breadth of canvas, grandiose in scale and in enterprise. In 405 he abandoned Gela, which he had been appointed to defend, and in the peace terms to which he then agreed Acragas, Selinus and Himera were ceded to Carthage and the rest of Sicily left free and neutral. Yet by 398 he had already overcome both Greeks and Sicels in eastern Sicily. With cynical disregard for Greek sentiment and with ruthless application of the only law under which he was prepared to act, that of his own interest, he destroyed Naxos, the oldest colony of all, handed Catana over to his Campanian mercenaries, and removed the people of Leontini to Syracuse. An energetic rearmament programme was set in hand, for which Dionysius imported metal-workers and shipwrights from all Hellas. Enthusiasm was tremendous, and we are told that the whole city resounded to the hammers of the smiths. From the concentration of so much talent resulted the development of catapults for the army and quadriremes and quinqueremes for the much-enlarged navy. Syracuse itself, after the lessons of the Athenian siege, was made almost impregnable. It was surrounded with new and massive fortifications, taking in the whole plateau of Epipolae, of which the most prominent and complex feature was, and still is, the fort Euryalus. Although remodelled to some extent nearly two hundred years later by Archimedes, Euryalus shows Dionysius to have had a remarkable and progressive approach towards city-defence and its possibilities.

Plates 43, 44

Fig. 11

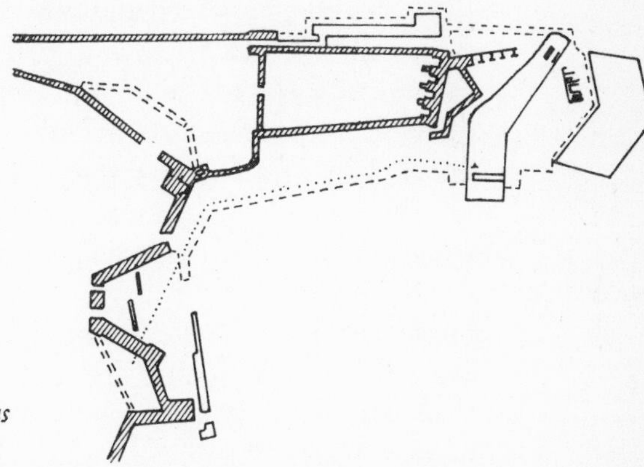

Fig. 11. Simplified plan of the Euryalus fort, Syracuse, after L. Mauceri

FIRST CARTHAGINIAN WAR

But if his ideas in defence were novel and courageous, he matched them with his methods of attack. In 397, with his eastern conquests secured, he reopened the war with Carthage, marched to the far end of the island, and captured the promontory-fortress Motya. In this siege the ingenuity of Dionysius' method and his use of siege-engines of a new and powerful kind were an immense advance on anything yet known in Hellas, and the desperation of both attack and defence remained unequalled until the generation of Alexander the Great and the sieges of Tyre and Rhodes. Yet in 396 the tide swept the other way. Himilco the Punic commander reached Syracuse from Panormus with little opposition from Dionysius, and the Syracusans were only saved by the outbreak of a plague in the Carthaginian army, the effects of which Dionysius assisted with a well-timed sortie. Although the war dragged on for three more years, the Carthaginians did not recover from this disaster, and their frontier with Greek Sicily was fixed henceforward as the river Mazarus, west of Selinus. In the second war Dionysius suffered a heavy defeat at Cronium and ceded territory west of the Halycus (*Platani*) by Heraclea Minoa, a situation which his final war did nothing to reverse.

Meanwhile, he waged a number of campaigns to subdue the Sicel communities. Enna and Herbita were among the earliest overcome; Cephaloedium and Morgantina were won by conquest, Centuripa and Agyrrhium by alliance. Tauromenium, founded by Himilco in 396 to dominate the site of the former Naxos, was repopulated with Dionysius' mercenaries. Messana which Himilco had destroyed, was refounded with settlers from Locri, and for a new colony, Tyndaris, the tyrant made use of Messenians from Greece. Control of Messana made it desirable to control Rhegium also, and since Rhegium called in Italian allies Dionysius became involved in a series of Italian campaigns. The result of these was that Rhegium and Croton were conquered, Locri (always a Syracusan ally) firmly held as a satellite, and Caulonia and Hipponium totally destroyed. Taras was his ally, and he even planted colonies at Issa, Pharos and Ancona in the Adriatic. Alliances with the Iapygians and Messapians extended his influence yet further.

Fig. 12

DIONYSIUS AND THE AEGEAN

Plate 45

Aegean Greece looked on at these achievements with admiration and distaste. Dionysius' alliance was enjoyed by Sparta and coveted by the Athenians, who did not achieve it until 368. He entered impressively for the Olympic Games where in 388 an attack on him in a speech by Lysias so inflamed the crowd that the Syracusan tents were set upon. Dionysius' chariots were unplaced in the big race and no one would give a hearing to his poems. His effective reply was to send a contingent to the Spartan fleet which blocked the Hellespont and compelled the Athenians to accept the King's Peace (386). The insult to his poetic gifts rankled particularly, for Dionysius

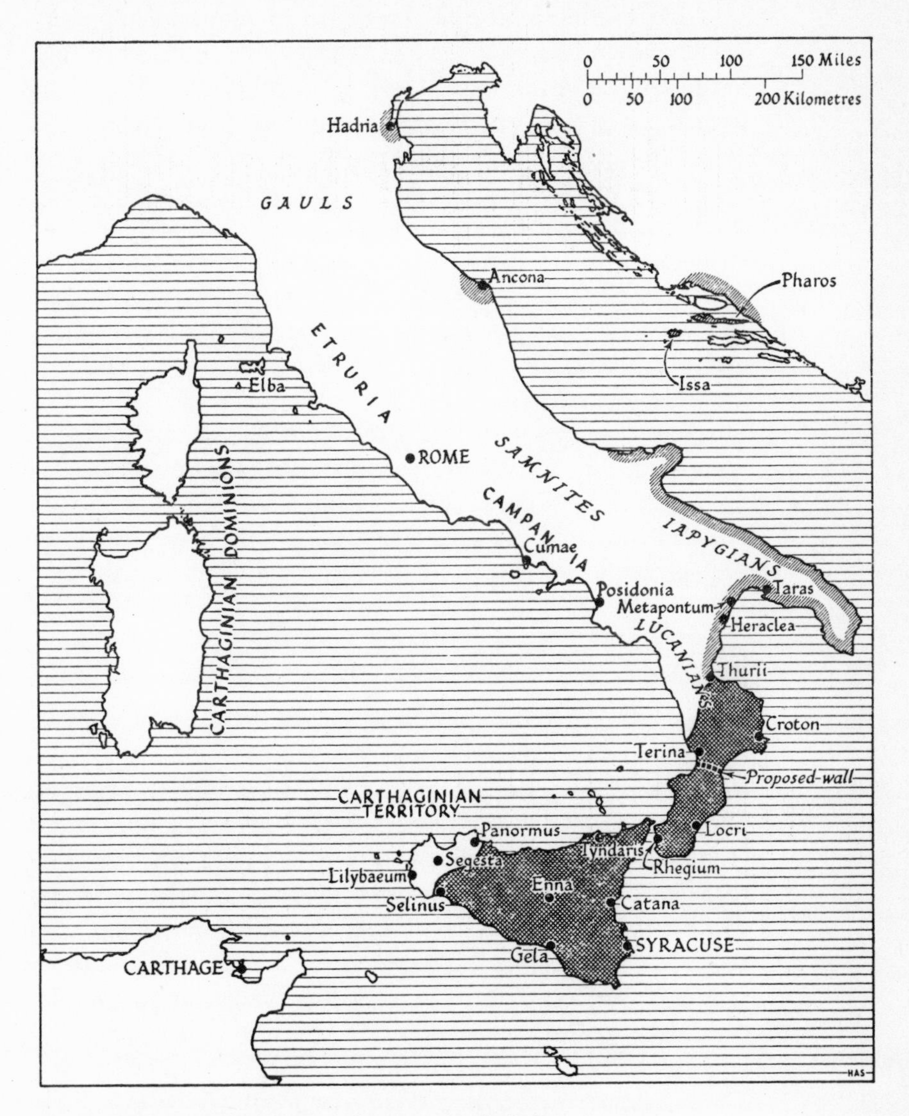

Fig. 12. The empire of Dionysius I of Syracuse, c. 380 B.C.

fancied himself a tragic poet. But, though he possessed the lyre, pen and writing tablets of Aeschylus or Euripides (it is uncertain which), his offerings failed to please the Athenian judges at the Dionysiac festivals. In 368, the year of their alliance, the Athenians became opportunely convinced of the merits of his latest production, *The Ransoming of Hector.* Dionysius celebrated his victory with such enthusiasm that he caught a fever from which he died.

In assessing Dionysius it would be unjust to make use of principles of moral judgement which he himself disregarded. He achieved with remarkable success everything he set out to achieve; his abilities as a military despot were great and undeniable. Isocrates envisaged him as the unifier of Greece, but Greece was more fortunate in Philip of Macedon, an abler and wiser man. The impact of Dionysius is tremendous and sometimes results in an overestimate of him. Closer and continuous study of his career suggests that there is only one facet to the brilliance and that the glitter even of that quickly tarnishes.

THE LIBERATORS

DIONYSIUS II

It says much for the popularity or efficiency of Dionysius' régime that on his death his son, now some thirty years old and also named Dionysius, succeeded without trouble to his position. Less ambitious and belligerent than his father, Dionysius II at once made peace with Carthage and gave other signs of relaxing the rigours of the tyranny. That so little is known of the first ten years of his reign, even through hostile channels, suggests that they were prosperous and uneventful: interest centres on his court where, as a result of Dionysius I's complicated matrimonial arrangements, he was surrounded by a number of ambitious relatives liberal with advice. Chief of these was

DION

Dion, brother of the dead tyrant's wife and husband of his daughter, a man of philosophical interests and a friend of Plato,

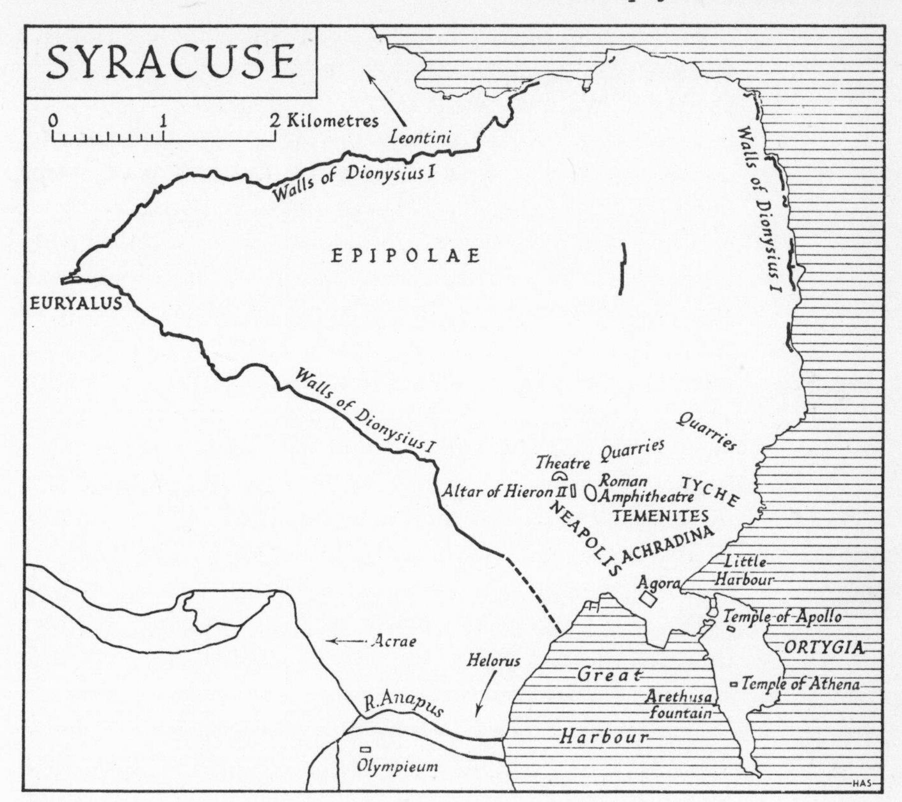

Fig. 13

whom he urged to come to Sicily and make of Dionysius II a practical example of the philosopher-king of his theory. Plato had made one unfruitful visit to Syracuse twenty years earlier; he now made two more, for though at first Dionysius seemed a promising pupil he was turned against Dion and Plato by a rival faction. Dion was exiled and Plato abandoned his task. But the philosopher's intervention had two effects on the tradition. Through his *Letters* he adds much to our scanty knowledge of Sicily at this time, and his connexion with Dion has secured for the latter a favourable verdict from history.

The study of Sicilian history in this generation must indeed, by reason of the biographic character of the material, be chiefly a study of two men, Dion and Timoleon. But although there is a superficial similarity between them, in that both were 'liberators', there is in fact a great contrast. Dionysius, in the tradition which Timaeus hallowed and which has been popular ever since, was a bad man; Dion and Timoleon were good men, and Dion had the additional qualification of being a tragic as well as a virtuous hero. During his exile he pursued his philosophic studies in Greece; urged in particular by Speusippus, he determined to restore liberty to Syracuse and destroy a tyranny which Dionysius II was now perpetuating without having either the character and ability to impose it or the popularity to be freely accorded it. Dionysius' enforcement of a divorce between Dion and his wife provided the final break. With a small force Dion sailed for Sicily, landed (by agreement with the Carthaginians) at Heraclea Minoa, marched at once to Syracuse and seized the outer city. Dionysius, who had been in Italy, returned and saved Ortygia, so that for some time Syracuse was divided against itself.

Plate 19

DION'S VARIED SUCCESS

Unfortunately Dion's connexion with the tyrannical house was a taint he could not shake off, and in an assembly drunk with liberation his rivals, especially Heracleides, made capital out of this. His political ideas also were too moderate for the extremer democrats; he lost popularity and withdrew to Leontini, while Heracleides, who had won a sea-battle against Dionysius' admiral, the historian Philistus, pressed the siege of Ortygia. A sudden counter-attack by Dionysius' Campanian mercenaries led to great slaughter in the lower city, and in despair the citizens sent for Dion. His swift triumph made him once again the popular hero, and Ortygia was soon surrendered by Dionysius' son, the tyrant himself having retired to Locri to continue the battle from there. But once again Dion lost his hold on the popular enthusiasm. He became a tyrant in spite of himself, and after having the obnoxious Heracleides assassinated he also was murdered (354 B.C.).

One tends to be suspicious of those whom history presents as models of rectitude. Dion undoubtedly had great personal qualities and unusual military ability, but his philosophy did not teach him the art of human relationships, and there are signs, not least his connexion with Carthage, which suggest that he was ambitious for power and applause but checked by scruples and fortunate in having respectable friends. His mismanaged 'liberation', however well-intended, condemned Syracuse to another decade of bloodshed and oppression, in which one tyrant followed another. Dionysius' tyranny alienated even the faithful Locrians, at whose hands his wife and daughters suffered a savage fate when he returned (346) to Ortygia, and in the outer city of Syracuse, we are told, all was neglect and decay. The tyrants' efforts to reinforce the Syracusan population had made of it a mixed and unstable body. Now, diminished in number and bereft of its empire, it looked for another liberator, more successful and more tactful than Dion had been.

THE SYRACUSANS APPEAL TO CORINTH

At this low point of misery, and with fears of a Carthaginian attack, the people of Syracuse appealed for help to Hicetas, a Syracusan who had made himself tyrant of Leontini, and to their mother-city, Corinth. Hicetas intrigued for a Carthaginian alliance, planned to make himself master of Syracuse, and wrote to Corinth that help was no longer needed; but Timoleon, a man of proven character though aloof from politics, had already been appointed to lead a rescue expedition. With nine ships and a thousand mercenaries he eluded a Punic fleet to make a successful landing at Tauromenium, where he was well received by the tyrant Andromachus, father of Timaeus the historian. With this small force he was to rid Syracuse of Dionysius, the Greeks in general of Hicetas and the other tyrants now so widespread amongst them (Andromachus being a single and honourable exception), and almost the whole island of the Carthaginians, whose policy now seemed to envisage complete annexation of Sicily.

SUCCESSES OF TIMOLEON

The story of his success reads like a romance in which justice triumphs and in the last chapter everyone seems destined to live happily ever after. Timoleon, his work completed, did not return to Greece as Gylippus had done, but lived in honoured retirement among the grateful Syracusans, who at his death built near the modern Piazza Marconi a Timoleonteum to commemorate him. It was a hero-worship he amply deserved.

After his arrival events quickly ran his way. At Adranum he was drawn into a faction-conflict in which he utterly defeated Hicetas, and Dionysius, whom Hicetas had been besieging on Ortygia, suddenly surrendered to him and withdrew to live out his days in Corinth. Timoleon then had a winter in which to prepare to liberate the rest of Syracuse, and although Hicetas was heavily reinforced by Carthage the liberator's own enterprise and his enemies' mistakes enabled him to accomplish this with speed and success. When, two years later, the Carthaginians sent another large army to regain Sicily, Timoleon though with inferior forces overwhelmed them near Segesta beside the river Crimisus (*Belice*?), the opportune flooding of which greatly helped him to deal with the more heavily armed Punic infantry. Subsequent but less important attempts by Carthage to combat Timoleon's success only supplemented the lesson of this battle. In 339 she was reconciled to the loss of all Sicily east of the Halycus.

NEW LIFE FOR GREEK SICILY

In the meantime Timoleon tackled the problems of population and government in liberated Sicily. His restoration of the moderate 'democracy of Diocles' in Syracuse was no doubt the model for other cities, and all Greek Sicily was united in some form of confederation. Quite apart from the general depopulation which the island had suffered, the Italic element had become very strong, chiefly as the result of the settlement of mercenaries. A colonisation programme of staggering dimen-sions was set in hand. Publicity in Aegean Greece, where a large colonising 'potential' still existed, as well as in Magna Graecia, where the future seemed less promising, brought new settlers in large numbers to reclaim abandoned land for cultiva-tion and to maintain the Hellenic character of the cities. Gela and Acragas were now founded anew, and Syracuse itself re-ceived no fewer than 60,000 new citizens, according to the contemporary Syracusan historian Athanis. The defences of Gela, Tyndaris and other places, and new civic buildings in Gela and Morgantina, testify to the importance of the *età Timo-leontea* in reviving city-life and liberty in Greek Sicily after the oppression and depression of the previous seventy years.

Plates 46, 47, 59
Plates 50, 51

Why did Timoleon succeed where Dion had failed? He was a very different sort of man from Dion; he had the ability to make himself popular while at the same time keeping an effec-tive control of affairs, in a way that Dion had not, and he was more sympathetic than Dion towards democratic ideas. He had no personal connexions at Syracuse to jeopardise his position there, while the Syracusans for their part were more chastened than ten years earlier. His hostility to Carthage was bitter and uncompromising, and he was ruthless in his opposition to the tyrants, to whom he showed a savagery in some contrast to the general mildness and amiability of his nature. His dealings with Mamercus of Catana, with whom he was at first in alliance, Hippon of Messana, Nicodemus of Centuripae and others, and with Hicetas most of all, may throw doubt on his much-stressed humanity. But his propaganda was good. The 'Timoleon-legend', which may be credited in the main to Timaeus, per-haps went back to Timoleon himself, and he mixed with it a modest and mystical dependence on fortune and the gods the importance of which was also realised by leaders of the stature of Scipio Africanus and Augustus. He has understandably been compared with George Washington, and though one may temper the judgement of history it would be perverse to deny it. Timoleon's few weaknesses may serve to underline the solidity of his virtues and his achievements.

AGATHOCLES AND PYRRHUS

ITALY IN THE FOURTH CENTURY

The extension of Dionysius I's empire into Italy had further weakened the Greek cities there, and once his tyranny had fallen they were ill equipped to face a new threat to which they were now exposed—a strong and cohesive Bruttian power. The Bruttii had previously been subject to the Lucanians, who in Dionysius' time had been the chief danger. Indeed Dionysius, using the Lucanians as allies for the defeat of Thurii, had turned on them with a decisive victory at Laüs (389 B.C.) and had contemplated the building of a wall across the isthmus at Catanzaro to keep them at a distance. But the Bruttii now proved a more immediate problem. From their new capital Consentia (*Cosenza*) they soon came to dominate a number of Greek cities. No help was forthcoming from the Tarentines. Although her temporary inclusion in Dionysius' empire had not impaired Taras' pre-eminence among the Greek settlements, the pressure of the native tribes caused her citizens to appeal for aid to Sparta. But while King Archidamus II in 342 hoped to do for Taras what Timoleon was doing for Syracuse, a three-year campaign ended in his defeat and death. More successful was Alexander of Epirus, uncle of Alexander the Great, who in a series of campaigns defeated not only the Messapians but also the Lucanians, Bruttians and Samnites. He showed signs of converting southern Italy into a personal empire, and the Tarentines turned on him in order to preserve their own liberty. A confused situation was resolved by his assassination.

INTERVENTION OF ROME

Both Greeks and Italians were, however, threatened by a new power to the north, that of Rome. A Roman agreement with Carthage (348 B.C.) had inaugurated Rome's advance into southern politics. Alexander and later the Tarentines made treaties with her, and by 326 conquest or alliance had brought Naples and the other Greek cities of Campania under her control. For the next generation she was involved in a bitter struggle with the Samnites, but her final victory, coupled with the defeat of the last great Gallic invasion (295 B.C.), left her in a position of dominance which the Greek cities feared but with which, unsupported, they could not argue.

SYRACUSE AFTER TIMOLEON

The respite which Timoleon brought to the turbulence of Sicilian history did not last long. The Sicilian Greeks did *not* live happily ever after. Once again they proved unable to use with wisdom and moderation the freedom which had been won for them, and the tyranny under which they now fell seems to have been more savage and rapacious than any of its predecessors. Much must perhaps be discounted in the details of Agathocles' career, as they are transmitted by Diodorus, for Diodorus drew largely on Timaeus, and Timaeus, whom Agathocles exiled, is at his most bitter and vitriolic on this particular subject. Even Diodorus himself, not normally so critical, admits to some hesitation—'in fairness one ought not to credit the last five books of this historian, in which he deals with the activities of Agathocles.' Nevertheless he preferred it to more favourable accounts, such as those of Agathocles' brother Antander or his court-historian Callias, preservation of which might have raised our estimate of what emerges as a period of tragedy, suffering and gloom.

Timoleon's moderate democracy became oligarchic in tone under the guidance of an aristocratic party of the Six Hundred. We hear of a war against Acragas, now flourishing anew, and an expedition to help Croton against the Bruttians (325). But these are recounted as incidents in the rise to power of Agathocles, whose father had migrated from Thermae (*Termini Imerese*) when Timoleon called for new settlers for Syracuse (343). Agathocles was then aged eighteen; soon afterwards he distinguished himself against Inessa and later in the Acragantine war. He made a wealthy marriage, and was already an important officer on the Bruttian campaign, while Antander had been elected general. Intrigue against the oligarchs led to his exile and a period as a *condottiere* in southern Italy. He saved Rhegium from a Syracusan attack, and this induced the Syracusans to recall him and expel the oligarchs. A war ensued against the exiles and their Sicilian allies which he conducted with some ability, but he withdrew when a Corinthian, Acestorides, was summoned as a second Timoleon to settle Syracusan difficulties. On Acestorides' return to Corinth Agathocles, from his exile at Morgantina, soon overthrew the restored oligarchy and was absolute ruler of Syracuse for the next twenty-eight years (317–289 B.C.). At first 'supreme commander', as Dionysius had been, he took the title of king in 304, in imitation of Ptolemy, Seleucus, and his other powerful contemporaries in the east, who at that time gave up the pretence of holding their shares of Alexander's conquests in trust for Alexander's successors. The change of name affected neither his supremacy nor the oppression with which he exercised it.

AGATHOCLES AS TYRANT AND KING

The exiled oligarchs lost no time in raising a Sicilian coalition against him, enlisting a Spartan named Acrotatus as their leader. But the allies fell out with one another, and by 312 Agathocles was able to capture Messana and a number of lesser cities, exterminating his opponents on each occasion without mercy or scruple. His success had alarmed the Carthaginians, hitherto content to observe the *modus vivendi* arranged with Timoleon. Thus they supported Acragas when Agathocles attacked it and in 311 they sent a large force under Hamilcar for a final reckoning with the Syracusan tyrant. Agathocles entered neutral Gela, slaughtering all who opposed him, and met Hamilcar at Licata, where in the battle of the river Himeras (*Salso*) he was heavily defeated. The Carthaginians now advanced on Syracuse and besieged it (311–10).

INVASION OF AFRICA

But Agathocles showed resource and inspiration in the crisis. While Syracuse, protected by Dionysius' fortifications, could weather the storm for some time, he resolved to draw Hamilcar off by attacking Carthage itself. With a small force he slipped out of the harbour, crossed to Africa, and won useful successes there. The siege of Syracuse was raised, and Agathocles, fortifying a base near Cap Bon, prepared for a long war. An alliance with Ophellas, autocrat of Cyrene, was wrecked by mutual distrust and Ophellas was murdered, but internal discord in Carthage very nearly played into the tyrant's hands. However, the Carthaginians pulled themselves together. Agathocles had to return to Sicily to deal with trouble there, and in his absence his sons were defeated and the Greek position was gradually undermined. On his return to Africa Agathocles judged the situation hopeless, abandoned his expedition, and made good his own escape to Sicily.

WARFARE IN SICILY

Meanwhile Hamilcar had made another attempt to besiege Syracuse (309) but had been defeated, captured and executed. Trouble came not from Carthage but from a league of 'free' cities organised by Acragas and led by Deinocrates, a Syracusan enemy of Agathocles. The struggle went on until 305, by which time the 'free' cities had been captured and their forces overcome by battle or bribery. Even Deinocrates himself was persuaded to serve under Agathocles. All of the cities save Acragas now came under his control. By this time, indeed, the old distinctions of Greek, Sicel and Elymian scarcely applied; all alike had been weakened by years of war, destruction and execution. The people of Segesta, for instance, not quick enough to pay a war contribution were butchered either outright or after horrible torture. Nor did Agathocles stop at allied blood. After his flight from Africa his troops had murdered his two sons before making what terms they could with Carthage. At this news, the tyrant ordered Antander to round up all the soldiers' relatives in Syracuse, and these, men, women and children alike, were herded down to the seashore and slaughtered forthwith.

AGATHOCLES' RULE IN SYRACUSE

Peace with Carthage restored the old frontiers in Sicily (306), and thereafter less is known of Agathocles' rule. He intervened in Italy, held Croton for a time, and even captured Corcyra. His reputation and importance caused his friendship to be sought by the Greek kings. His third wife was Theoxena, daughter of Ptolemy I of Egypt, and his daughter Lanassa married first Pyrrhus of Epirus and later Demetrius Poliorcetes. Family animosities, however, frustrated his attempts to form a dynasty, and at his death he 'restored Syracusan freedom'. But his own career had made any sort of popular government impossible. Murder and execution ensured that his sons and grandsons did not survive him, and the Syracusans industriously destroyed his statues and other monuments.

So bare a summary can do little justice to Agathocles' restless and kaleidoscopic career, which exercises a macabre fascination. History may have given him less than his deserts. Despite the methods of his control, some of which have an uncomfortably modern echo in their refined efficiency, his tumultuous reign ably matched the tumultuous epoch in which he lived, and imposed some sort of order in the chaos of Sicilian strife. One might even venture to suggest that the Sicilian Greeks, miserable with him, would have been more miserable without him.

SICILY AFTER AGATHOCLES

Agathocles' death in 289 B.C. threw Sicily into new confusion. His long and active despotism left no abiding mark save the impoverishment and weakness of the Sicilian cities, which were now a ready prey for any adventurer who could impose himself on them or any foreign power ready to seize the opportunity. A new crop of tyrants arose. Phintias of Acragas removed the population of Gela, which he destroyed, to the site of Licata, where he founded a new city bearing his own name. His successor Sosistratus carried on a war against Thoenon of

Syracuse, while the Carthaginians, who over long years had had little abiding success in their attempts to gain control of all Sicily, intervened with enthusiasm undiminished to profit as best they could. Agathocles' mercenaries, too, had formed a power of their own, seizing Messana and calling themselves *Mamertini*, 'sons of Mamers' (Mars). A Carthaginian fleet sailed to attack Syracuse in 278, but Sosistratus and Thoenon urgently joined their forces and appealed for help to Pyrrhus, king of Epirus, now campaigning in Italy on the invitation of the Tarentines.

Fig. 15

ROME AND TARAS AT WAR

Taras' difficulties with the Italian tribes had continued unabated after Alexander's intervention, but the leaders whose assistance they sought proved almost as barbarian as the enemy. Cleonymus of Sparta (303) had fallen foul of the Metapontines and had withdrawn after a defeat at the hands of the Lucanians. Agathocles won temporary successes against the Bruttians, but his sack of Croton had left the more vivid memories. Small wonder that Thurii asked for the support of the great power to the north, Rome, which had just emerged triumphant from a long war against the Samnites and which, through a Lucanian alliance, was now the preponderating influence in southern Italy. This was little to the Tarentines' liking. They regarded themselves as protectors of the Italian Greeks, and their dealings with the Romans hitherto had shown some *hauteur*. A treaty existed which excluded Roman ships from their waters, and when in 281 ten Roman ships did appear off Taras they were set upon. Not content with this, the Tarentines marched to Thurii and forced its Roman garrison to surrender. Rome demanded satisfaction, and the Tarentines, adding to Roman injuries insults to their envoys, prepared for war, inviting the Epirot king to lead them. Pyrrhus, after a chequered career, had made Epirus into a large and powerful kingdom, and was eager to accept an invitation which offered booty, glory and adventure. As a soldier he was reckoned by no less a judge than

Fig. 14. Bronze plaque from the sanctuary of Zeus Naios at Dodona, commemorating the victories of King Pyrrhus over the Romans, 280–279 B.C. The letters were formed by a series of punched dots

Hannibal to be second only to Alexander the Great. He could therefore hope to succeed where the native Italians had failed, and with the sophisticated *expertise* of Hellenistic military art to halt the rapid advance of the Romans.

ITALIAN SUCCESSES OF PYRRHUS

Some cities, including Locri and Rhegium, had joined Thurii in accepting Roman garrisons, but when in a battle at Heraclea (280) Pyrrhus defeated a Roman consular army they had second thoughts. The king was confident, from his experience with Greeks, that Rome's Italian allies could also be persuaded to change sides, and he marched to within forty miles of Rome itself, only to find himself in country unwaveringly hostile. In the next year he again defeated the main Roman forces: but though at Asculum the Romans lost their consul Decius Mus and 6,000 men Pyrrhus' victories had been expensive, and in Greece trouble and opportunity alike made him regret his commitment. The appeal from the Sicilians prompted him to accept tentative terms with Rome and cross the straits; but the negotiations were inconclusive, and in his absence the Romans secured, by capture or treaty, all the Greek cities in Italy save Taras.

Fig. 14

PYRRHUS IN SICILY

Hailed as king of Sicily, Pyrrhus set about clearing the whole island of Carthaginians, and soon had them penned into their old territory in the far west. He crowned this remarkable achievement of speed and skill by the capture of Mt Eryx and of the fort Heirkte overlooking Panormus. But the difficulties of a siege of Lilybaeum wearied his patience and his allies' resources, and the Carthaginians began to recover after their early setbacks. In 275 he abandoned the Sicilians and returned to Italy, recapturing Locri and Croton on his way to meet a renewed Roman threat. But by now his position was less strong, and at Beneventum he was decisively beaten. He had little to show for his six years of western adventure, and on his withdrawal, though he left them a garrison, the Tarentines' surrender was inevitable. By the end of 272 all of Greek Italy was in Roman hands.

Plate 36

The Roman terms of surrender and alliance were generous, and under Roman rule the Greek cities enjoyed a security they had never known. But their sufferings, especially during the recent war, left them weak and, in the larger context into which they were now absorbed, of minor account. Posidonia was freed from the Lucanians and refounded as a Latin colony: Taras alone was garrisoned. At Rhegium Roman power now looked across the straits to Sicily, and it was not long before the Romans were drawn into the continuing maelstrom of Sicilian affairs.

THE INDIAN SUMMER OF SYRACUSE

HIERON II OF SYRACUSE

Pyrrhus' adventures left Sicily more or less in the state in which he had found it. The Carthaginians regained all the territory in the west and centre of the island that they had lost, and the Mamertines in Messana carved out a little empire for themselves in the north-east. The remaining section of the island continued under the rule of the Syracusans, for whom Agathocles'

Fig. 15

ex-mercenaries proved troublesome neighbours. Under a new general, Hieron, they met at first with no success, but later captured Halaesa and Tyndaris and, but for the timely provision of a Punic garrison at Messana, would have destroyed the Mamertines' power altogether. Hieron was proclaimed king, as Hieron II, by a grateful people, and thus began a long reign of fifty years (265–215) in which, as the most untypical of the Syracusan despots, he guided his city benevolently through the fruitful autumn of her independence.

Fig. 15. Copper coin of the Mamertini, showing (obv.) Ares laureate and (rev.) eagle with thunderbolt: drawn from an example now in the Fitzwilliam Museum. Cambridge

ROME AND THE MAMERTINI

But the Mamertines, rid of Hieron, had no wish to become subject to Carthage, and their recent defeats left them unable to act without assistance. Their obvious move was to appeal for help to the new power across the straits, and the Romans after much hesitation, though barely recovered from the war with Pyrrhus and its aftermath and despite early treaties with Carthage, decided to respond with an expedition into Sicily. It is hard to see what advantages the Romans expected to get: the Mamertines were weak and distasteful allies, and Rome was in no danger from either Carthage or Syracuse. There was no 'inevitability of conflict'. But the tide of success had been flowing strongly for the Romans. While some may have feared Carthage more than they need, others may have hoped for new opportunities of honour or booty, and the whole citizen-body was perhaps buoyed up by their Italian conquests. With the crossing of the straits of Messina in 264 they took their first step on the path of overseas empire, and in Carthage they faced the major obstacle to domination of the western world.

THE 'FIRST PUNIC WAR'

The 'First Punic War' belongs more properly to the history of Rome, and a detailed narrative of it is out of place here. It is for us more important to ask what happened to the Sicilian Greeks, ground between the upper and nether millstones of Rome and Carthage. Whatever happened, they could hardly fail to be the losers, and the fate of most of them would depend on the victors' generosity. Most difficult of all was the position of Hieron, for whom the preservation of an independent Syracusan kingdom was a delicate problem. The circumstances of the war's origin made him an ally of Carthage—a strange situation for a Syracusan leader—and in 264 he withstood the attacks of the consul Appius Claudius. But the Romans were anxious to detach him from the Carthaginians, and in 263 with the capture of Tauromenium, Catana and other cities they came to Syracuse itself. Hieron realised where his interests lay and, having now seen something of the Romans in action, weighed up the relative prospects of the opposing powers. The treaty he now concluded with Rome for a term of fifteen years consolidated though slightly diminished his kingdom, which now reached from Tauromenium in the north to Helorus in the south. He took little further active part in the war, but the Syracusan harbours and repair-shops were open to Roman warships, and the fertile cornland which Syracuse controlled was useful as a source of supply for the Roman armies. In 247, when the treaty had run its time, it was renewed without limit and further territory was added to Hieron's kingdom, which now covered about a quarter of Sicily. Hieron and Syracuse in fact did well out of the war, and the city settled down to the most tranquil period of its independent existence.

MISFORTUNES OF THE SICILIANS

Elsewhere in the island some cities, such as Enna and Camarina, suffered severely, seized now by one side and now by the other, and punished by both for surrenders they could not have avoided. Their lands were devastated, their economy ruined, their strength in people and possessions dissipated. Others seem to have emerged largely unscathed. Early in the war the Romans struck at the west of the island. Accepting Segesta and Halicyae as allies they laid siege to Acragas; after five months a relieving Carthaginian army besieged the besiegers, but Hieron brought fresh supplies and after two more months the Carthaginians gave way. Acragas was sacked and its inhabitants sold as slaves, *pour encourager les autres.* The effect of the Roman success was to confine Carthage to her old possessions in the far west. To shorten their defences they removed the Selinuntines to Lilybaeum; Selinus was destroyed, and its history, violent and chequered as it had been, was ended. With the failure of Regulus' expedition to Africa, in which the Romans fared no better than Agathocles had done, the war on land continued for fourteen weary years with little profit to either side, and for ten of those years Lilybaeum resisted a persevering Roman blockade. The decisive issues were fought on the sea, and the Sicilian coasts witnessed the great engagements which ultimately destroyed Carthage as a sea-power and settled the fate of the western world. That off Mylae was Rome's first naval victory (260), that off Cape Ecnomus by Licata was, for numbers, the largest fought in antiquity (256), that off the Aegatian islands (*Isole Aegade,* by Trapani) in 241 was the defeat which brought Carthage to surrender. The coast of Sicily was also the scene of one of Rome's greatest maritime disasters. In 255, in a storm off Camarina, 284 ships were wrecked out of a fleet of 364 sail—with an estimated loss of about 100,000 men or some fifteen per cent of available Italian manpower.

Rome fell heir to the former Carthaginian territories in Sicily. and after 241 ruled either directly or through treaties with 'free'

HIERON'S PROSPEROUS REIGN

cities the whole island outside the Syracusan kingdom. The Syracusans could thus have no adversaries and no ambitions. With confidence in Roman restraint Hieron gave his engines of war to the Rhodians and applied himself to the arts of peace. He rebuilt and extended the theatre to its present form and size; inscriptions still to be seen there show that the 'wedges' of seats were identified by the names, among others, of himself, his wife Philistis, and his daughter-in-law Nereis, who was the daughter of Pyrrhus of Epirus. At the back of the theatre he built porticoes and a Nymphaeum to which water supplies were led by aqueduct. His great altar east of the theatre, more than two hundred yards long, could accommodate a thousand animals for simultaneous slaughter. The whole area of Neapolis seems to have been remodelled, while on Ortygia the king had a fine palace later used as their Government House by the Roman praetors. His generosity enriched not only Syracuse but also

Plate 41

Fig. 16

Fig. 16. Northern end of the great altar of Hieron II at Syracuse (restoration of R. Koldewey and F. Puchstein, Die griechische Tempel in Unteritalien und Sizilien). *The altar was 199.07 m. in length*

Plate 49

the dependent cities within his borders, such as Acrae and Agyrrhium, with temples, theatres and gymnasia. At the end of his long reign Hieron left his city prosperous and splendid. Yet he himself lived modestly, and the Syracusan constitution functioned without restraint. Several times he offered to resign—offers which popular decree as often rejected. The last of the great Syracusan autocrats, he was from every human point of view also the best, and Greek Syracuse that survives is in the main the Syracuse of Hieron II.

HIERONYMUS

At his death in 215 he was succeeded by his grandson, the fifteen-year-old Hieronymus, his son Gelon having predeceased him by a few months. Roman disasters in the Second Punic War, culminating in the great defeat at Cannae (216), had made it seem that the future lay, after all, not with Rome but with Carthage. A pro-Carthaginian party had powerful support in the two chief regents, Hieron's sons-in-law Zoippus and Adranodorus, and negotiations with Hannibal's agents Hippocrates and Epicydes led to an agreement that Syracuse would join Carthage, the reward being dominion over all Sicily. Such a bargain the Carthaginians, if victorious, would have no need to keep, and it provoked a reaction inside Syracuse. Hieronymus and Adranodorus were murdered, and for a while it seemed as if the situation might be saved for Rome. But Hippocrates and Epicydes were elected generals, and raids across the border provoked M. Claudius Marcellus, the proconsul, into marching on Leontini (213), which had declared for Carthage independently of the Syracusan decision. The city was sacked, and Marcellus moved on to draw his siege-lines round Syracuse itself.

MARCELLUS AND THE SIEGE OF SYRACUSE

Syracusan determination was reinforced by the immense strength of Dionysius' fortifications, extensively remodelled by the ingenuity of the scientist Archimedes, whose engines of defence repulsed every Roman attack. The Romans were forced to settle down to a siege of attrition, and were diverted by a

Carthaginian army which had landed at Heraclea Minoa, captured Acragas, and advanced to Syracuse itself. Marcellus managed to hold the rest of Sicily apart from Morgantina, where the Carthaginian commander Himilco wintered with his army, but the Roman position in Enna was maintained only precariously by a slaughter of part of the population. The winter of 213–12 found the Romans in a generally uncomfortable situation.

In the new season, however, fortune became their firm ally. A plague swept away Himilco, Hippocrates and the Carthaginian army more effectively than the swords of Marcellus' legionaries could have done, and carelessness and cowardice on the part of the defenders allowed the Romans to get possession of Epipolae, Euryalus, Neapolis and Tyche. The fall of the remainder of Syracuse became a matter of time, and when in spring 211 the Carthaginian admiral Bomilcar failed to arrive with a relieving fleet dissension broke out among the Syracusans. A gate was opened, and Syracuse was taken and sacked. Cicero says that Marcellus, marvelling at the wealth and splendour of the city, showed remarkable restraint. It remained for later Roman governors, principally the infamous Verres, to rob the Syracusans of what Marcellus' troops spared. Among the victims was Archimedes, killed at his drawing-board while pondering a geometrical problem.

Fig. 13

SICILY A ROMAN PROVINCE

It took a further year of campaigning before the consul of 210, M. Valerius Laevinus, completed the pacification of Sicily with the recapture of Acragas. Messana, Tauromenium and Netum preserved a status of 'independent ally', and a few other places such as Segesta and Panormus had lesser privileges. For the rest, the island became a province administered by a praetor or, after *c.* 80 B.C., a propraetor or proconsul. The story of the western Greeks is finally merged in that of Rome.

Yet, although the history and fortunes of the Sicilian and Italian Greeks now became merged in those of Rome, they were by no means submerged. It is worth while to carry their narrative, even if briefly, to the foundation of the Roman Empire, to the time when Diodorus of Agyrrhium, writing his *Library of Universal History* (in Greek) in the reign of Augustus, could remark in his preface, 'By getting to know the Latin-speaking settlers in the island I have been able to acquire a thorough mastery of the Latin language.' For him Sicily was still a Greek island: but the settlement of which he speaks had been in progress for the best part of two centuries. Cicero in his speeches against Verres refers a great deal to Roman business-men and land-owners, many of whom suffered from the propraetor's rapacity no less than the Sicilians themselves. The aftermath of the civil wars increased the Roman element, and by the end of Augustus' reign it would be fair to regard the civilisation in the south as a new Graeco-Roman amalgam.

THE ITALIAN GREEKS UNDER ROMAN RULE

The Italian Greeks, who had been the first conquered, became part of the Italian system and were governed from Rome. The *Lex Plautia Papiria* of 89 B.C. gave them all Roman citizenship, so that their status thereafter is indistinguishable, but the original settlement of the time of Pyrrhus had not been ungenerous, and the Hannibalic War upset what seems to have been a thriving relationship. Successive Roman disasters caused the Bruttians to go over to Hannibal, and Taras, Metapontum, Thurii and other places followed suit (213). Taras, where the Romans managed to retain the acropolis, was recaptured and sacked four years later, and Rome gradually re-established her hold in the south, but it was from Croton that Hannibal was able to sail for Africa in 203, and the whole area was much devastated by the long war. The Greek cities declined to the point that only a transfusion of new blood could save them.

Colonies of Roman citizens were established at Thurii, Croton and Vibo (Hipponium) in 194, and at Taras by C. Gracchus in 122. The civil wars of the Sullan period hit Campania hard, and Sulla planted colonies at Pompeii and Paestum in a general resettlement of the area. Bilingual inscriptions from these cities and from Velia illustrate the fusion of the two cultures within these Graeco-Roman communities.

Plates 52, 54

Large tracts of land in the south fell into the possession of wealthy *rentiers* who farmed them as *latifundia,* estates principally pastoral and worked by slave-labour. This agricultural pattern of large estates has persisted until recently, and the city-states in consequence of it became economic as well as political backwaters, favoured by metropolitan Romans for vacation or retirement. Horace mirrors the quiet relief of a man of affairs leaving for the peace and relaxation of 'Lacedaemonium Tarentum', and in Trebatius' villa at Velia, as a retreat from the grim realities of the times, Cicero had a friendly meeting with Brutus after Caesar's murder.

ROMAN SICILY

Sicily was from the start on a different footing, a *provincia populi Romani.* Its inhabitants received Roman citizenship in 44 B.C., a grant which Antony engineered on the basis of what he claimed to have been Caesar's intention. Before and even after that they had much to suffer in peace and war. Sicily as one of Rome's principal granaries was particularly important to the Roman economy, and its wealth not only in corn but also in wine, olives and other products, as well as in sheep and cattle, is repeatedly emphasised by the Roman writers. The ship-building and textile industries also flourished under the Roman republic. But, as in south Italy, the *latifundia* became the predominant pattern of land-holding, and the slave-population grew to be very large. The negligence of absentee landlords and the poor conditions under which many slaves were kept produced two great servile revolts (135–2 and 104–100 B.C.), in which there was much damage and loss of life. In the first, the

SLAVE REVOLTS

slave-leader Eunus, calling himself King Antiochus, controlled for a time Enna (where the inhabitants were massacred), Acragas, Catana and Tauromenium. The post-war settlement, the *Lex Rupilia,* produced a new charter for the province after an experience which affected the Romans deeply and contributed much to the movement of reform headed by the Gracchi. The latter revolt was concentrated more in the west of the island, around Heraclea Minoa and Lilybaeum. After these lessons the Romans reduced in number both the *latifundia* and the slave-population, and Sicilian prosperity is attested by the amount of loot which the infamous propraetor Caius Verres (73–71) was able to appropriate. Cicero's successful prosecution of him, undertaken despite every possible obstruction on the part of Verres' influential friends, on the urgent application of all the cities of Sicily save Messana and Syracuse, has preserved to us two speeches, the second, which is of great length, being divided into five books; in them the Sicily of 70 B.C. is graphically mirrored, and the sufferings of cities and individuals at Verres' hands are described in pathetic detail. Yet despite such temporary depredations the general prosperity of Sicily regained its stability, and its cities were populous and thriving. Cicero was pleased and proud to be considered its patron.

C. VERRES

A factor contributory to this healthy state of affairs, which even Verres had not been able to distort to his own advantage, was the equitable taxation-principle of the tithe. This had been the creation of Hieron II, and the Romans had extended the *Lex Hieronica* to the whole island. It was a fair tax justly assessed and levied, and Cicero speaks in glowing terms of Roman wisdom in preserving it. The régime of Verres and others like him had caused something of a flight from the land either to avoid their exactions or because of ruin as a result of them; but Sicily was too important to the government, and after Verres' condemnation a liberal policy of agricultural encouragement was at once set on foot with excellent results.

SICILY IN THE CIVIL WARS

Plate 55*b*, *c*

Although the Sicilians were little involved in the civil war between Caesar and Pompey, the seizure of the island by Pompey's son Sextus brought seven years of loss and trouble. Antony and Octavian, busy elsewhere, had to acknowledge in 39 B.C. Sextus' right to possession, but when in 36 Agrippa landed at Tyndaris to expel him the ensuing campaign ruined Messana, Tauromenium and the whole of the north-east. Octavian in landing at Naxos came as near to disaster as ever he did, and the fortunes not only of the Greeks in the West but of the whole Roman empire were determined by the caprice of fate at the spot where, seven hundred years earlier, so much of the story had its beginning. Sextus escaped to the east, plundering the temple of Hera Lacinia at Croton on his way, and left Sicily to the difficulties of reconstruction and to the blessings of the imperial *pax Romana*.

Plate 7

CHAPTER V

The Achievement of the Western Greeks

POLITICS AND THE CITY-STATE

TIMAEUS THE HISTORIAN, though he spent much of his life in Athens, was a man of ardent patriotism who grasped at every opportunity to emphasise the contribution to civilisation which the Greeks of Sicily and Magna Graecia had made. Hence his particular interest in systematising the Greek legends to the benefit of the west. No contribution was too humble for his purpose. He remarks for instance that part of the noted 'luxurious living' of the Sybarites consisted in their invention of vapour baths and chamber-pots—which latter, he adds, they used to carry with them to parties. In the attempt to assess, in the pages that follow, the contribution that the Greeks in the west made to what may be summed up in the word 'Hellenism', it is important to avoid chauvinism of this kind, lest a latter-day Polybius echo his predecessor's remark that 'to Timaeus' way of thinking anything that happened in Sicily was more important than all that happened everywhere else in the world put together.' Nevertheless, the development of the Western Greeks was in many respects very different from that of their brothers to the east. They were faced with different problems, and even in the handling of ideas (whether political, philosophical or artistic) shared by all the Greeks their answers were often distinctive and unusual. Their contribution, in its differences as well as in its agreements, thus forms an integral part of the whole picture of Greek civilisation.

The difference of problem and answer is nowhere better exemplified than in the development of the city-state and its government. The *polis* as the governmental unit, in ideal and in practice, was the common heritage of classical Greece. Its form of government was usually aristocratic or oligarchic. The heavy preponderance of our information about Athens leads the unwary at times to the notion that the Athenian democracy was typical of city-states throughout the Greek world. On the contrary, though it had imitators from time to time, no other city—so far as we know—which attempted a democratic system matched its success and its quality of administration, so that both its form and its conduct should more properly be thought of as atypical. But whether an oligarchy or a democracy the city-state in Greece was by itself a weak unit, unable to resist a strong centralised power with substantial resources in men. Lack of ability to create workable combinations of *poleis,* in which liberty could be found compatible with co-operation, made the situation worse, for the cities wasted their strength and resources in conflicts with their neighbours and in the attempt to create city-state empires—the only kind of *polis*-coalition which seemed to be effective.

All this was in a sense a luxury, and the Greeks who indulged in it were living on borrowed time. A critical moment had come with the Persian invasions, but with mingled skill and luck the defenders survived the challenge of the world's greatest military power. Thereafter, for more than a century, the city-states could develop without an external threat. Persia never again became a serious danger and Macedon, though a useful barrier against northern invaders, did not develop its latent strength until the middle of the fourth century. When it did so, the classical city-state could not long survive.

The Western Greeks did not enjoy these unthreatened years in which their cities could blossom in all the endeavours of the human spirit, unhampered by anything save their own inherent shortcomings. Once the colonies had taken root, the constant pressure of the Carthaginian menace or of the tough and belligerent Italian tribes did not allow them to achieve an equilibrium. Their own tendencies to mutual distrust and discord added to their difficulties, for they inherited all the characteristics of jealous parochialism and ambitious imperialism to be seen among the Aegean Greeks. The fifth century, in which these external pressures grew to be at their most formidable, tended as a result to divert the western *poleis* into expedients of authoritarianism, even though in many of them a sound constitutional basis, in advance of the general Greek development of the time, had been laid in the tradition of Zaleucus and Charondas. The alternation of dictatorship and liberty in Syracuse, and the violence of each, is a feature of *polis*-history unparalleled in the Greek world, and the failure of Syracusan democracy is as worthy of study as the success of its Athenian counterpart.

The resilience of oligarchy, no less evident in Aegean Greece, remains a constant factor in the west. Assailed from time to time by autocrats and democrats, it provided Syracuse with her intermittent periods of stable government, and in the 'hundred families' at Locri, where some form of matriarchal system also survived, or the intellectual élite of Pythagoreans at Croton provided as dependable a régime as these cities seem to have had. In other instances evidence is insufficient to show any clear development; but all the Italian cities whose history is known in any detail came to require the services, which in the event amounted to the domination, of a supreme commander, whether he came from Sparta, Epirus or Syracuse.

The story of the Western Greeks is thus not only illuminating, as it was to Plato and Aristotle, for its picture of the follies of democracy and its often-repeated examples of the fall into the abyss of the worst system of all, tyranny. It shows the Greek *polis* exposed to all the trials from which the accidents of history protected the cities of the Greek peninsula, and with this revelation of its deficiencies we may be helped to shed that prejudice of sentiment which, when we look at Greece alone, may sometimes hamper our judgement.

In an earlier chapter reference was made, in connexion with Selinus and Acragas, to the 'Hippodamian' system of urban development, that of a chessboard or 'grid-iron' of streets dividing regularly planned blocks and having equidistant right-angled intersections. Such a system may, but need not, include two principal axial thoroughfares, the intersection of which will mark the centre and chief business area of the city. Hippodamus of Miletus, active in the fifth century, is credited chiefly on the basis of two references in Aristotle's *Politics* with having discovered this principle of town-planning, and he is said to have laid out the Piraeus, Thurii and Rhodes in accordance with it. But although the supposition is still to be met with that before Hippodamus Greek cities were haphazard and unplanned growths, and that he produced a revolution in Greek thinking on this subject, it has been increasingly realised that his rôle cannot have been more than that of a developer, perhaps a populariser, of a system known and used long before his time.

see pp. 51, 53

The earliest evidence for axial planning in a Greek city now comes from Smyrna, where in the early seventh century houses with a consistent north-south orientation clearly attest a master-plan. But it is in Sicily and Magna Graecia that the majority of early examples of the Hippodamian town-plan are to be found. One or two of them may indeed antedate the Smyrna example, and while in at least one instance the early date of the 'grid-iron' layout has been challenged the weight of evidence elsewhere is strong enough to suggest that in any disputed cases such a plan could well be original. Since the cities laid out by the *oikistai* were built *de novo,* with no inherited proprietorial or religious obstacles to a practical division of the territory on a regular principle, it was the easiest and most natural plan to form a series of rectangles in so far as the terrain allowed. This system is now visible at Acragas and may be supposed, on the basis of the later plan, for Selinus. It is also clear at Casmenae, and Posidonia, though little of its great area has been excavated, appears to follow the same pattern; here the level ground made it easily practicable.

Plate 57

Aerial survey has recently made an important contribution to this study, and from the air the grid-iron plan of Metapontum has now been recognised. A similar plan has also been identified at Caulonia, but it may be the plan only of the city as rebuilt after its destruction by Dionysius of Syracuse (389 B.C.); if so, the nature of the site nevertheless suggests that the rebuilding may well have followed the previous plan. Not all cities were susceptible of such treatment. While it is likely that Sybaris and Croton were axially planned, and in the fifth century Thurii certainly was, it is hard to see that Velia could have been laid out in this way, and the early section of Syracuse, on Ortygia, can have followed a Hippodamian system only to a limited extent. What is more, certain sections of cities otherwise planned on the chessboard system could not for geographical reasons be included in it. At Acragas, for example, the acropolis could only be laid out as a series of terraces, and the religious sanctuaries of the city bear no relation to the street plan of the residential area—a contrast with Posidonia, where they could be accommodated to the over-all plan without difficulty. At Selinus the land falls away round the acropolis, interrupting the plan; but the temples on the Marinella plateau are clearly laid out on an axial system. The careful planning of the agora at Morgantina has revealed to its recent excavators that Greek Sicily also took the lead in an aspect of town-planning which Hellenistic and Roman architects were to develop to great effect.

Fig. 17

Fig. 6

Plates 50, 51

Further study, from the air and on the ground, will no doubt develop our knowledge of the city-plans of the Greek colonies wherever circumstances allow, for this clearly offers a fruitful field of much-needed research. What has already been achieved

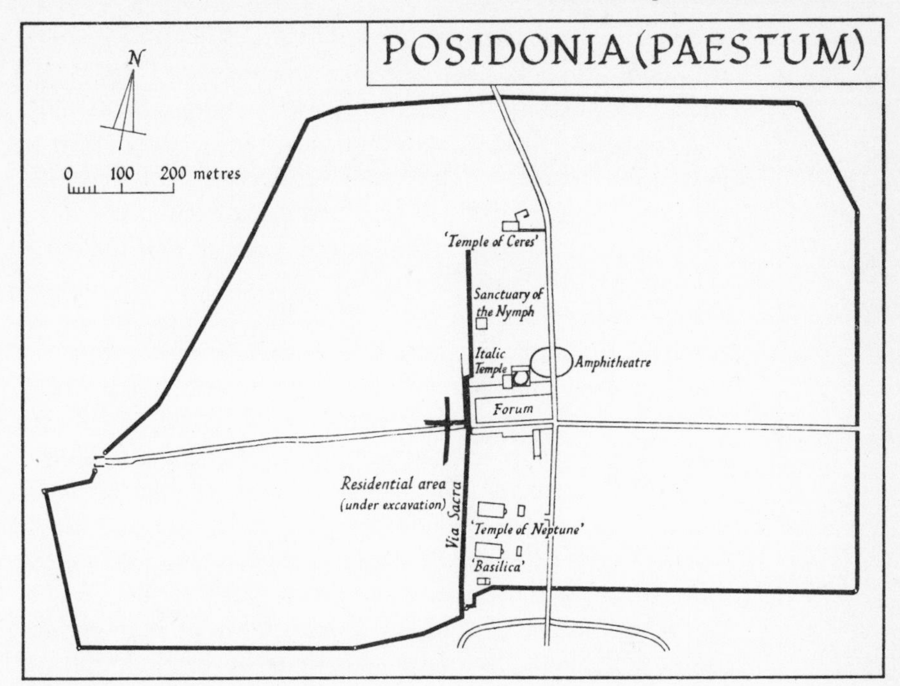

Fig. 17

seems to be controverting recent argument that this archaic evidence is insufficient to deny Hippodamus and Ionian town-planning their due credit. At least it can be said that the contribution of the Western Greeks enables us to look to an earlier period in the development of Greek society than the often-repeated diagrams of Miletus and Olynthus for regularity of pattern and for the application of a master-plan firmly and effectively carried through.

ARCHITECTURE IN THE WEST

The Greek colonists carried westwards with them the general architectural standards, ideas and predilections current at the time, and there was always sufficient movement between east and west for the Western Greeks to share fully in the important developments in architectural style and technique during the archaic and classical periods. Master-architects were never numerous, and those known by name in the tradition were in international demand. The builders of the great monuments in Italy and Sicily are likely to have had direct or indirect contact with the best contemporary examples. Yet they were not afraid of experiment and innovation, and although their ideas did not always 'come off' they reflect a readiness to make a fresh approach to accepted architectural patterns. Even the treasuries which some of the western cities built at the sanctuaries of Olympia and Delphi emphasise, in their use of western materials and motifs, their vigorous independence of treatment.

The well-worn remark that more Greek temples are to be seen in Sicily and Italy than in Greece itself, true only if one counts what is substantially above ground, draws attention to the importance of this part of the Greek world for the study of Greek architecture. For certain aspects of it, for example, the study of terracotta revetments, it cannot be bettered. But the most obvious and best-known monuments, the large temples, span little more than 150 years. After 400 B.C., the west has little to offer. The temple of Asclepius at Acragas, of Hellenistic date, is small and without a surrounding peristyle, and the less well preserved Temple B at Selinus and the Serapeum at Tauromenium were similarly unpretentious. What is more, apart from the religious sanctuaries, with which should be in-

Fig. 18

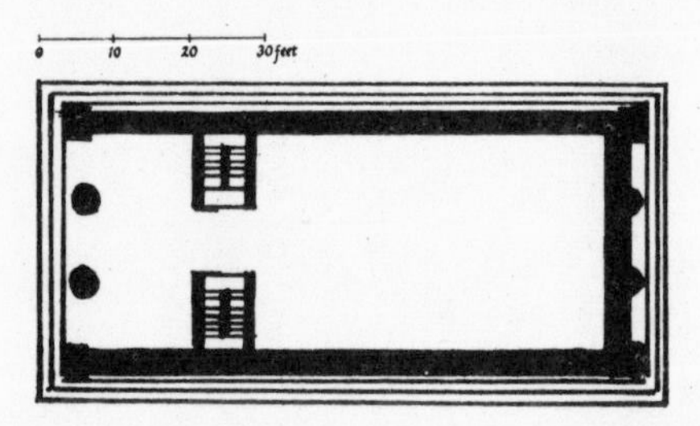

Fig. 18. Temple of Asclepius at Acragas: ground plan

cluded such constructions as the altar of Hieron II, little monu-mental architecture of this kind survives at all. The theatres are discussed below: work is in hand on the residential sections of a number of cities, Posidonia, Elea, Acragas, Morgantina and Tyndaris among them, which will add usefully to the much-needed study, little developed as yet, of domestic architecture: at Acrae a small council-house is preserved; walls and fortifi-cations are of an importance and impressiveness to deserve special treatment. But otherwise, of stoas and colonnades, of naval arsenals and port buildings, of palaces and palaestrae, there is barely a trace. The one-sidedness of the western legacy, whatever its cause, is worth observing.

Fig. 16

Plate 49

AGORAS

Of western agoras, only that at Elea is known in any detail, and the greater part of that belongs to the city's Roman phase. The Paestan forum seems to be an introduction of the Italic period into what had been an exclusively sacral area. Elsewhere, continuity of occupation has made it impossible to recover much of the ancient site. At Gela, for instance, the main piazza appears to be the modern counterpart of the ancient market-square; at Syracuse the Piazza Marconi marks the site of the agora and Timoleonteum, with a Roman theatre not far away. At other sites, for instance Tyndaris, the same is probably true. Morgantina is proving a fruitful excavation in this respect, its agora carefully planned with flanking stoa and theatre, and with its two levels united by a monumental stairway; but in other now deserted sites, such as Locri and Selinus, the agora has not been identified.

Plate 57

Plates 50, 51

TEMPLES

The development of techniques meant that in the west, as in Aegean Greece, the standard architectural practices varied with time. Thus to the use of polygonal masonry for the city-walls of the sixth century was added the regular ashlar, often isodomic, of the fifth and fourth. The plan and layout of the majority of the temples corresponded, at least in principle, to those familiar elsewhere in the Greek world. The use of stone for the upper

Plates, 8, 46, 47

structure came, as in Greece, to replace wood and terracotta, though surviving remains of the earlier technique fill out our knowledge of a stage less well evidenced in Greece itself. On the other hand, the Western Greeks, lacking good marble, seem to have made less use of sculpture as decoration for metopes and pediments, even though the richness of their terracotta facings and akroteria suggests that they enjoyed a brilliant decorative effect. It is possible that in general they preferred the grandiose to the graceful, so that their decorative schemes appear overdone.

Although many of their decorative elements, and indeed the size of some of their projects, suggest that they had plenty of contacts, direct or indirect, with Ionia, the architectural order which they used was almost exclusively Doric. Locri and Hipponium offer the only examples of Ionic temples *in situ*, though an Ionic porch lurked behind the Doric peristyle of the 'Temple of Ceres' at Paestum. But, just as archaic Athens used the Doric order for buildings but enjoyed the Ionic on dedicatory or commemorative columns standing by themselves, so in the west there is plenty of evidence of the popularity of Ionic motifs. A capital from Selinus seems to belong to just such a columnar dedication, and early examples from Acrae, Gela, Syracuse and Megara Hyblaea show a variety of treatment which offers some of the best evidence for the development of the Ionic order. The *caduceus* commemorating the Thurii-Brundisium alliance has an Ionic volute to decorate it; Ionic capitals are found on Tarentine tomb-monuments, and Ionic columns appear on the Persephone-plaques from Locri. In the course of time some local variation was introduced into the canonical Ionic capital, as is illustrated by a 'Siculo-Ionic' example from Centuripae.

Plate 20
Plate 23
Fig. 10
Plate 66

The 'Corinthian' capital, an invention of the later fifth century, appears in its earliest form at Bassae, not yet stabilised into a standard pattern, and this is followed early in the next century

Fig. 19. Capitals from late fifth- and early fourth-century tombs at Taras: redrawn from H. Klumbach, Tarentiner Grabkunst, *plates 31 and 33. The largest of the capitals shown here is 20.8 cm. high*

by examples at Delphi and Epidaurus. Yet Taras can offer samples of Corinthian capitals in tomb-architecture which suggest that at an early stage the Western Greeks adopted and began an independent development of this new architectural form.

Fig. 19

In the details of plan, construction and decoration of their Doric temples the Western Greeks not only tended to differ from Eastern Greek practice but differed also from each other. It is hardly possible in face of such diversity to speak of 'Sicilian Doric' or 'Italian Doric', and attempts at discussion are liable to become catalogues of western eccentricities. Nevertheless, the 'deviations' are in themselves illustrations of western willingness to experiment and corresponding unwillingness to become constricted by a rigid formula. The local stone, generally limestone, which the western builders used did not admit of the fine precision which their eastern colleagues were able to achieve with marble; yet they made up for this by superb stucco work delicately painted, as has been recently evidenced at Selinus. They did not seek the refinements in angle and curvature of which the Parthenon is the most notable example, but they produced in the 'Temple of Neptune' at Paestum one of the most 'regular', in plan and measurement, of all Greek temples. The surviving upper storey of its internal colonnades also provides the sole remaining western example of this device for dealing with the interior height of the roof.

Plate 64

The Western Greeks may have adopted from Ionian models the devices of enlarging the centre intercolumniation on the 'approach-side' of a temple (as in that of Apollo at Syracuse), and of deepening the entrance-portico by inserting a second cross-colonnade running between the third columns of the long sides of the peristyle, as in Temples C and F at Selinus or the early Syracusan temples. The internal arrangements also differed from what was usual in Greece, many temples having a plain rear wall and no opisthodomos opening on to the peristyle. In

Fig. 20

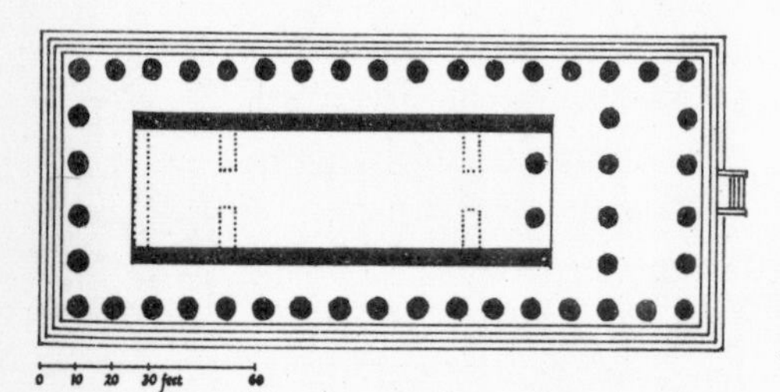

Fig. 20. Temple of Apollo at Syracuse: ground plan

the 'Temple of Ceres' at Paestum a cella of this kind has a prostyle porch, but such a porch is combined with a regular opisthodomus in Temple G at Selinus. The temple of Apollo Alaeus at Crimisa (Cirò) was unusual in several respects, having a plain rear wall, a deep portico at both ends and without additional cross-colonnades, and within the cella a single rather than a double row of columns, with four columns arranged in a square in the adyton. The single row of internal columns, indicative of early date, is found also in the 'Basilica' at Paestum, where it is matched, however, by an uneven number of columns (nine) on the short sides of the peristyle.

Plate 23

Plate 24

The early builders at Syracuse seem to have mistrusted the capabilities of their columns. In the temple of Apollo these were set closely together and tapered sharply from bottom to top, so that the building, long though it was, must have looked squat and heavy. Triglyphs were normally set above each column and intercolumniation, but here, at least at the ends of the temple (where in contrast with normal Greek practice the intercolumnar spaces were narrower, rather than wider, than those on the long sides), they were apparently set only over the columns, leaving a long metope between. This elongated metope, apparently evidenced at Taras, is also found over the porch of the 'Temple of Ceres' at Paestum, a building which in the construction of the entablature over the peristyle was also peculiar. Plate 23 The architrave blocks did not span each intercolumniation but rested their centres on the columns in a cantilever arrangement. The triglyphs above them were not separate blocks but were formed of slabs grooved into the blocks forming the metopes. Decorated mouldings above and below this metope-triglyph frieze, combined with the omission of a 'floor' to the pediment, made the whole concept novel and rather striking. The pediment roof was also unusual in its decoration of coffers, each with a star at its centre. In this temple and in the 'Basilica', as well as in the Heraeum at Foce del Sele, there was some experiment Plate 63 with the Doric capital. The junction between shaft and echinus was decorated with a leaf-pattern, and on some of the Paestan *Fig. 21* capitals the echinus itself carries relief-decoration.

Freedom of treatment of the frieze and cornice is further illustrated in the pentaglyphs from the Marafioti temple at Locri and *Fig. 7* the peculiar use of the terracotta regulae and guttae at Crimisa, where two rows of these are added, in a staggered series, to the *Fig. 22* raking cornice of the pediment. This arrangement Dinsmoor condemns as barbaric, but it shows a vigorous and uninhibited approach and may have looked well. The junction of the cornice with the pediment floor appears less successful, and the

Sicilian terracotta cornices also found difficulties at this point which were not satisfactorily surmounted. It is worth while to

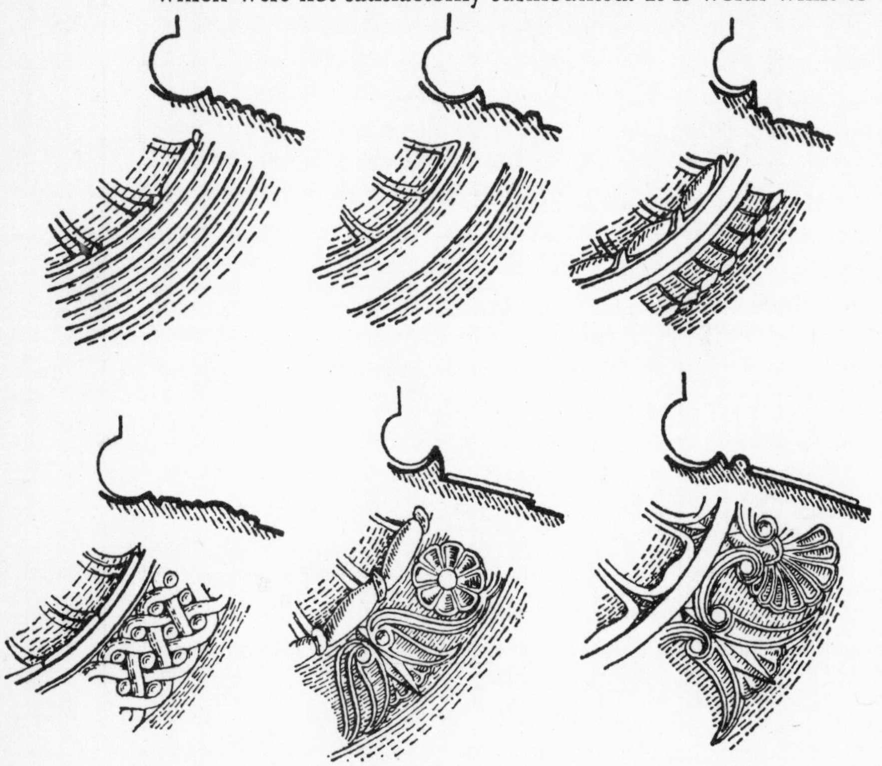

Fig. 21. Six examples of decoration on the echinus of Doric capitals in the 'Basilica' and 'Temple of Ceres' at Posidonia (Paestum)

add that the moulding of western Doric buildings reflects an interesting blend of Doric and Ionic models.

The pronounced entasis of early western columns is one of the features which evokes particular comment. This is so obvious that it cannot have been intended to correct an optical illusion—a suggestion put forward to explain the 'invisible' entasis on the columns of the Parthenon. It may have been a tentative aesthetic solution to the heaviness of the early Syracusan examples; if so, the device cannot be said to have failed.

Finally, a word should be said of the radical innovations of the Olympieum at Acragas and the western experiments in size, beginning with the great length of the Syracusan temple of Apollo and culminating not only in the Olympieum just mentioned but also in the enormous Temple G at Selinus, the stylobate of which measured no less than 50 x 110 metres.* Both these latter were perhaps too large for adequate roofing and may have been compluviate, that is to say, had an interior open to the sky. Here again the Western Greeks showed an almost transatlantic tendency towards the grandiose for its own sake and the boldness of their concepts claims respect and admiration.

THEATRES

Concerning theatres in the west space permits no more than a few summary words. That at Syracuse was one of the earliest permanent buildings of this kind in all Hellas; its Hellenistic remodelling occurred at a time when an enthusiasm for theatre-construction seems to have gripped the Sicilian cities. Most of

Plate 40

Fig. 22. Cornice of the Doric Temple of Apollo at Crimisa (Cirò)

the theatres were adapted in Roman times to more modern forms of entertainment, as may be seen at Syracuse and Tyndaris, but the theatre at Tyndaris was originally constructed in the Hellenistic period, and the stage-buildings at Segesta also

Plate 56
Plate 10

* For comparison, the Parthenon measures on the stylobate some 30 x 70 metres.

show a remodelling early in the Roman period (*c.* 100 B.C.) of a Hellenistic original. The theatre at Acrae, again Hellenistic, foreshadows Roman fashion in reducing the auditorium to an exact half-circle; that at Tauromenium is, as it stands, purely Roman. At Heraclea Minoa the theatre (now more precisely known from recent excavations) seems to be an unmodified building of the early third century, while similarly at Morgantina, where the newly discovered theatre has been dated by its excavators to the fourth century, the decline of the city eliminated the need for subsequent modification. Of the Massalia theatre little is known, but the seating is clearly enough of the Greek pattern; a theatre has also been under recent excavation at Locri.

Plate 30

Theatres were used not only for dramatic performances but often also for political assemblies. Their frequency in the western cities re-emphasises the liveliness, both cultural and political, of the communities they served.

WARFARE AND FORTIFICATIONS

The inter-city battles of Greek *polis*-rivalry were usually fought out by the better-off citizens themselves, wearing heavy body-armour and helmet, and equipped with shield, spear and short sword. Drawn up in opposing masses, normally eight ranks deep, the two sides hacked away at each other until the weight and strength of one of them prevailed. The only variant of this pattern was the Theban device, employed most effectively at Delium in 424 and Leuctra in 371, of giving one section of the line extra weight by a deeper formation. Such was the 'regular' battle; but it was of course always possible to take the enemy unawares, in ambush or before he had formed up, or to overwhelm a detachment with a massive superiority. For ambush and skirmishing, especially the picking-off of irregulars and foragers, cavalry was much used, but not until Alexander the Great welded it into a striking force was it effective against a hoplite phalanx. In the city-state it lacked numbers and training. It was the prerogative of the wealthy, and oligarchies, usually well-provided, deployed it chiefly against each other.

In such circumstances walled cities were practically impregnable to assault save by some trick of stealth or surprise. Starvation and treachery, or the despair of the besieged, were the main weapons. The time and expense of the Athenian siege of Potidaea (432–29) or the Spartan siege of Plataea (429–27) are sufficient illustrations of the poverty of the classical Greeks in this branch of warfare. Even the great Athenian siege of Syracuse was, as far as siegecraft was concerned, a sorry affair.

In the fourth and third centuries progress was made, and in it the Western Greeks took no small part. In earlier days the pattern of western warfare had resembled that in Greece, though the excellence of the Sicilian and Italian plains for the rearing of horses had enhanced the use of the cavalry arm, while the wealth and political needs of the fifth-century tyrants had developed the services of the more efficient professional soldier, long before the mercenary became a part of the Aegean scene. This was helped by the ready availability of Italian troops, especially Campanians, and one consequence of this early 'professionalism' was emphasis on a growing brutality and thoroughness in dealing with the enemy. Greek *polis*-animosities were no less bitter in the Aegean than in the west, but old Greece did not see the warfare *à outrance* displayed as early as the sixth century in the destructions of Siris and Sybaris and continued thereafter by such masters of the art of total war as Gelon, Dionysius I and Agathocles. While they do not seem to have been tactical innovators in the infantry-battle itself, the great Syracusans showed a leadership and efficiency in the conduct of war, and a shrewdness in judging the time and place of attack, which transformed the city-state concept of 'magistrate-generals' in stressing the superiority of the king or tyrant as supreme and professional 'war-lord'.

See p. 91

Plates 46, 47, 59

Emphasis has already been laid on the importance of Dionysius' capture of Motya in the history of siegecraft. That this was not noticed in his own generation is evident from the mid-fourth-century writer on military matters, Aeneas Tacticus. For Aeneas, in discussing city defence, takes no account of Dionysius' great siege-towers and catapults—the latter new inventions with which he had been able to make the besieged keep their heads down while his towers approached and overtopped the curtain-walls. Defence, however, kept pace with innovations in attack. The contrast for instance between the walls of Posidonia and those of Tyndaris or other 'Timoleontean' fortifications indicates that a greater strength and height, with the use of projecting towers to enfilade the attacker, helped to make a successful siege once again as difficult as it had been. Timoleon himself had no siege to face, and all that is known of him as a commander in the field shows him as striking when the enemy was at a disadvantage. He seems never to have fought a 'regular' battle, and Agathocles' defeat at the river Salso was no orthodox affair but a struggle for possession of the Carthaginian camp. In Africa, though he won a regular engagement, Agathocles knew that only treachery could deliver Carthage to him. His assault on Croton owed its success to surprise.

Plates 43, 44
Fig. 11

By the time of the Second Punic War city-defence was still the superior of regular attack. The northern defences of Selinus, remodelled in the mid-third century, show on a smaller scale an ingenuity similar to that displayed in the final phase of Euryalus. There the strength of the mounts for the Syracusan artillery and the complexity of the gates, moats and tunnels are the finest surviving monument of Greek military science. The effectiveness of the catapults, mechanical grabs and engines to carry and drop heavy weights which Archimedes devised show, from Polybius' description, that the Romans were justified in deciding to 'do anything rather than try to take Syracuse by assault'. The balance which a Syracusan had challenged by a development of assault technique was redressed by Syracusan perfection of fortifications and defence machines. Until the invention of gunpowder, Archimedes had the last word.

EXPLORATION IN THE WEST

The voyage of the first Mycenaean trader who found his way to southern Italy, Sicily or the Lipari Islands was as much a venture of exploration as of commerce. The same might be said of the Greek adventurers who, eight or nine centuries later, first prospected the shores where the colonists, following in their wake not long afterwards, planted their new settlements. Yet of these journeys and of the people who made them nothing is known. The early *oikistai* were not explorers in the accepted sense, for they depended on the exploratory work of others. Even Protis and his Phocaean followers at Massalia seem to have followed where anonymous Rhodian parties had led. Of the early merchant venturers one is known who became an explorer by accident. This was Colaeus of Samos, whose story is told by Herodotus, and from the historical circumstances to which it is attached his voyage seems to have taken place *c.* 650–30 B.C. On a journey to Egypt he was met by persistent easterly winds which blew him westwards through the straits of Gibraltar, beyond which he succeeded in making harbour at Tartessus, west of Cadiz. This port and its trading possibilities, though familiar to Phoenician traders, had remained beyond the Greeks' range, and Colaeus was able to return to Samos a wealthy man as a result of his unexpected fortune.

COLAEUS

But the route to Tartessus and the intensive exploration of the western end of the Mediterranean, set in hand particularly by the Phocaeans, were interrupted by the Carthaginians, as has been described. They not only began to drive the Greeks out of Spain but closed the straits of Gibraltar to all traffic but their own. Greek knowledge of the farthest west began to grow dim, and there was no possibility of improving it. Tartessus was destroyed *c.* 500 B.C., and perhaps soon after that date came the western voyages of Himilco and Hanno, the latter of whom is thought to have penetrated as far south as Sierra Leone. It was presumably *via* Carthaginian traders that the Greek coins found in the Azores and the pottery from Mogador in Morocco reached their destinations.

After a gap of some three centuries the Carthaginian iron curtain was briefly raised and the next Greek who ventured into the far west was also the greatest of the Greek explorers—Pytheas of Massalia. His voyage took place in the last quarter of the fourth century, and his account of it gave rise to controversy from the very start. It has been suggested that he sailed west between 310 and 306, when the Carthaginians were too busy defending their territory against Agathocles to keep the straits adequately guarded. Beyond them Pytheas turned north, where the details which he plotted as accurately as he could long served as the basis for maps of northern Europe. The uncertainty as to whether, in following the Carthaginian 'tin-route' to the 'Cassiterides', he kept close to the Gallic coast or struck directly across the Bay of Biscay may have been to some extent clarified by the discovery of a Cyrenean gold coin of 322–313 B.C. on a beach near Brest, in circumstances suggesting that it was lost overboard or by shipwreck when it had not long been in circulation. It is tempting to associate it with Pytheas' company on their way to Land's End.

PYTHEAS IN THE FAR NORTH

The party circumnavigated Britain, which Pytheas described as triangular, giving measurements of its sides, and then passed northwards to the most controversial part of the journey—the approach to Thule, where there 'is neither sea nor air, but a mixture like the substance of a jellyfish', a day's sail from the frozen sea. Thule may have been Iceland or Norway: the particulars Pytheas gave would suit either, though the mixed sea and air have been considered especially suitable as a description of a clammy sea-mist appropriate to the Norwegian coast not far from the Arctic Circle. Returning south, Pytheas made his way into the Baltic and seems to have reached the mouth of the Vistula. An island where he found amber, which the natives collected on the shore, used for fuel was possibly Heligoland.

After the return of this Hellenic Columbus no one ventured to follow where he had led, and so much turned on his credibility, which was immediately challenged by his contemporary Dicaearchus. He certainly made errors in his calculations of distance, and many details of his story were derided by the critics, chief among whom in the surviving record were Polybius and Strabo. But Timaeus believed him, and Eratosthenes, the greatest of all the Hellenistic geographers, while hesitating on certain points accepted the general truthfulness of his account. It now seems agreed that Pytheas' voyage not only happened but happened in the way Pytheas said it did.

It remains to mention one further Greek explorer of the west, Eudoxus of Cyzicus (late second century B.C.). By this time it had come to be believed that Africa could be circumnavigated, and Eudoxus, who made two successful voyages from Egypt in the direction of India (which indeed he may have reached), had the idea of finding a route there round Africa which would avoid the frustrations of dealing with the Egyptians. But his attempt to anticipate Vasco da Gama miscarried. On his first voyage down the west African coast he does not seem to have gone beyond Dakar, if as far; from his second, neither he nor his company returned. By this period, however, the growth of the Roman empire, with its expansion to the west and north-west, was beginning to alter the whole complexion of geographical research in the region of the Atlantic. To that research, it must be confessed, the Greek contribution had been limited, but the voyage of Pytheas remains its one fascinating and magnificent gesture.

Most of the western colonies were founded and took root in what has been described as the 'Lyric Age' of Greece. Though the life of the pioneer might reduce the possibility that lyric poets would arise in the west to match the talents which the well-established societies in the east were able to elicit, it was not impossible that Taras might produce a western Tyrtaeus or Alcman, Megara Hyblaea a new Theognis, or Siris a western counterpart to its mother-city's Mimnermus. In fact, however, the Muse worked in unexpected places. Two western lyric poets were enshrined in the Alexandrian 'canon' of nine, and the home of the greater genius of these, Stesichorus, was at Himera. He may have been born in Italy, at Metaurum, and his career seems to span the seventy years 630–560 B.C. His principal works were narrative poems on epic themes but in lyric metres. That on Heracles and the cattle of Geryon has already been referred to: others, on the Calydonian boar-hunt, on the Agamemnon story and on Helen of Troy, were also famous. His poetry combined grandeur with imaginative interpretations of old themes, and his 'twist' to the Helen legend was later developed in Euripides' *Helen*.

STESICHORUS

See p. 28

IBYCUS

Ibycus of Rhegium belonged to the next generation, although his work, less impressive than that of Stesichorus, was originally of the same character. He left Rhegium, apparently for political reasons, and removed to Samos, where he changed the manner of his poetry and began to produce love-songs for the court of the tyrant Polycrates. It was the warmth and brilliance of these which made his reputation, though the fragments of his work are regrettably scanty. His heart seems to have remained in the west, and after his death (the story goes that he was killed by robbers) he was buried at his native Rhegium.

THE PHILOSOPHER POETS

The philosophers Xenophanes, Parmenides and Empedocles should also be mentioned at this point, for they expressed their ideas in poetic form: Empedocles in particular rivalled as a poet his fame as a thinker. Scholarly interest in poetic development emerges with a work on the early poets written in the reign of Dionysius I by Glaucus of Rhegium.

Stesichorus and Ibycus lived too early for the patronage of the great Deinomenid and Emmenid tyrannies. For the proper eulogy of their victories in the Greek games, Hieron and Theron called on the services of the Boeotian, Pindar, some of whose greatest odes were inspired by his Sicilian connexions. Bacchylides and Simonides also are known to have been welcome visitors to the west. Two hundred years later the court of the second Hieron gave a start to the career of Theocritus, though he soon deserted the literary backwaters of the west for the greater attractions of the Aegean and Alexandria.

THEOCRITUS

DRAMA

But the artistic interests of the Syracusan tyrants in particular led to a substantial western contribution in the field of drama. Among the customs which the settlers transplanted were the religious ceremonies of their original homes, some of which included dances in honour of the god. Athenaeus mentions women's dances in a fertility-rite of Artemis Chitonea at Syracuse which seem to have paralleled similar ritual in the Peloponnese. It is likely that from songs and narrative which accompanied such choric performances both tragedy and comedy gradually developed. Arion, the Corinthian dithyrambic poet who is regarded as the father of the tragic drama, was an early visitor to Italy and Sicily and may have influenced Stesichorus. In their turn Aeschylus and perhaps Euripides travelled westwards, and Hieron's theatre, one of the earliest permanent structures for dramatic performances, assured the tragedians of the warm reception and first-class presentation of their work. Aeschylus' *Aitnaiai* was written specially for this theatre and dealt with a local theme. But the western theatres, which came to be numerous, staged the work of the great Attic masters and had little western talent to draw upon. Dionysius I was

Plate 41

probably a better dramatist than a hostile tradition gives him credit for, and it is perhaps worth adding that his son inherited some of his poetic gifts—being mentioned in particular as a writer of paeans. The dearth of dramatic talent was, however, general; nowhere in the Greek world could post-Euripidean tragedy offer anything to rival what had gone before.

COMEDY

It was in comedy that western Greece laid the foundation of a new art-form. Comedy itself took a line different from that at Athens, where the political 'old' comedy was a stage the west did not go through. The festival-processions, especially those connected with fertility-rites, produced a comedy of everyday life played by grotesquely-clad actors, which approached more closely the type of the 'new' comedy familiar from Menander. Though Aristoxenus of Selinus is the first name associated

Fig. 23. Circe threatened by Odysseus and Elpenor (or Theano threatened by Odysseus and Diomedes): a pyhlax-scene from a bell-krater in the Museo Jatta, Ruvo (Apulia)

with this kind of drama, Epicharmus, a Syracusan and contemporary of Hieron, was its greatest exponent. His plays contained no chorus, and while some took their comic situations from legend, quoted fragments show a wide range of subject and characterisation. After him Sicilian comedy developed no further, but his plays probably had some effect on the future course of its Athenian version.

MIME

More important as a western innovation was the mime. This developed from *ad hoc* performances, mostly by way of caricature, into character-vignettes and short dramatic episodes. Sophron of Syracuse (mid-fifth century), who is particularly associated with its early stages, and his son Xenarchus wrote more in the vernacular than Epicharmus had done. This kind of entertainment acquired great popularity, as the *phlyakes*-vases testify, and was exported to the east. The mimes of the Hellenistic Herodas survive to illustrate what was made of this art-form by the Alexandrian poets.

Fig. 23

THE WESTERN HISTORIANS

Although the Western Greeks had their independent problems and pursued independent careers to an extent that much of Aegean Greek history could be written with little reference to them, Hellas remained the single world which is the theme of this book, and the west was from time to time vitally involved in pan-Hellenic affairs. Herodotus and Thucydides were compelled to devote part of their histories to the west, and for the latter in particular his Sicilian sections were of major consequence as the hinge of Athenian fate in the Peloponnesian War. Later writers of the history of their own times, such as Theopompus and Polybius, found the west as important for their work as the east, while for writers of universal history such as Ephorus it was equally indispensable. However, we are concerned here not with Greek historians of the west in general but with westerners who wrote about their compatriots, and it would not be unjust to omit Herodotus from their number despite his residence at Thurii for some years after its foundation.

HIPPYS

There was little Greek historiography before Herodotus, and the earliest western historian was a younger contemporary of his named Hippys, a Rhegine, of whom nothing is known. It is in fact an obstacle which a discussion such as this must face, that nothing survives, save in quotations by other authors, of any western writer of history except the last in the period under review. What we know of them we know at second-hand, and their quality we must judge from their use by others as source-material, their recorded reputation, and our estimate of the quoted fragments when these can be isolated. Thus the history of Antiochus of Syracuse, which dealt with western affairs from Kokalos to the Conference of Gela and was still read in Augustus' day, underlies much of Thucydides' Sicilian information and was clearly an important work. So was that of Philistus, the faithful minister of Dionysius I and II, whose championship of the Syracusan tyranny evoked criticism and controversy among subsequent writers. Described by Cicero as a 'pint-sized Thucydides', his style was somewhat harsh and the critic Dionysius of Halicarnassus found him sometimes difficult to follow. Nevertheless, he formed part of Alexander the Great's travelling library.

ANTIOCHUS

PHILISTUS

ATHANIS AND OTHERS

Of Philistus' fourth-century successors little can be said. The tyrant Dionysius wrote history as well as tragedy: there are a Sicilian, Alcimus, cited once or twice for sociological details, and the Syracusan, Athanis, of whose thirteen books of *Sikelika* three quotations remain. Athanis' work certainly included the career of Timoleon, and he seems to have been involved in politics as a democratic opponent of Dion. Of the writers of Agathocles' generation Callias and Antander have already been mentioned. Lycus of Rhegium dealt with western as well as African affairs, and in the Hellenistic period Andreas of

See p. 101

Panormus studied the antiquities of Sicily city by city. A Syracusan, Nymphodorus, also wrote on 'Sicilian Marvels', but is chiefly quoted for information on other parts of the Greek world.

TIMAEUS

Such large-scale disappearance of these and other writers may be chiefly accounted for by the effect on the tradition of Timaeus of Tauromenium, already much quoted in these pages. Whatever may be said (and his ancient critics said a great deal) of Timaeus' shortcomings as a historian, he overshadowed and replaced his predecessors, and later writers who wanted to use a western source turned to him. Although he lived in Athens for fifty years of a long life, and is censured for being too much of an armchair historian, he allied to his enthusiasm for the Western Greeks a love of chronological exactitude and a perseverance especially in unearthing documentary evidence which aroused even Polybius' favourable comment. He also included in his *History* an account of early Roman history, and since he cannot have died long after the outbreak of the First Punic War this was foresight indeed. Quotations from him outnumber those of all other western historians put together, and reveal a breadth of interest which strong and sometimes intemperate partisanship does not spoil. The criticism provoked by this latter characteristic, which accounts for many of the recorded extracts from his work, may result in some one-sidedness in our knowledge, and study of him leaves the impression that his reputation with posterity has been less than he deserves.

DIODORUS

More than two centuries later Diodorus of Agyrrhium settled down to write a *Library* of world history in forty books, which was a patchwork of his predecessors' material. He wrote for a public which apparently looked for no more than a historical digest, without caring for style or literary quality, and his importance lies in the fact that, like the Abbé Siéyès, he survived: at least, fifteen books remain intact, and there are fragments of twenty-one more. His qualifications for his task were far inferior to his enthusiasm, and although it is useful to see through him to the character of the sources, now lost, on which he drew, his incompetence all too frequently serves only to confuse the issue. It is a cruel trick of fortune that the surviving representative of western historiography should be one whose claim to the honour seems so comparatively slender.

WESTERN PAINTING

The almost total loss of large-scale Greek painting has restricted our knowledge of the Greeks' mastery of this two-dimensional art-form chiefly to the painted decoration on their pottery. The value of their pottery-styles and development as archaeological evidence has already been emphasised: the classical archaeologist must count a thorough knowledge of the subject among his primary obligations. But we are here concerned with vases as artistic products, and in particular with those which were popular in the west. It will appear that while the Western Greeks adapted Aegean traditions, as they had done architecturally, with a fresh and lively approach of their own, the bulk of their products were inferior to their (principally Attic) models, though surpassing the imitations which the Etruscans and the Italic peoples began to produce for themselves.

COLONIAL TRADITIONS

The colonists continued to import good pottery from their Greek homeland as long as good pottery was produced there, and its popularity with the Greeks themselves and their Etruscan neighbours meant that Italian tombs were, in the early days of modern archaeological study, the chief source of 'Grecian urns'. Work at such sites as Spina and Felsina continues to illustrate the intensity of trade in fine vases during the period of Athenian pre-eminence in that field. But the Greek settlers soon began to make pottery for themselves, and some of it was a reasonable copy of popular wares, as for example at Ischia, where the colonists produced fair imitations of the then prevailing Protocorinthian. In Sicily a local pottery with geo-metric and orientalising motifs was developed, some of the best coming from the Syracuse area. The Geloan ware which is illustrated is in just such a tradition. But pottery was also made for the native market in no way reminiscent of the styles the Greeks had left behind.

Plate 16

Plate 15

PONTIC AND TYRRHENIAN

In the north the Etruscans tried to imitate for themselves the Corinthian and later the Athenian types which they welcomed as imports. Some 'Italocorinthian' is very competent, and the best kind of Etruscan black-figure vases, the so-called 'Pontic', the speciality of which was the neck-amphora, is not infre-quently pleasant and lively. But the Etruscan craftsmen tended to tinker with shape, style, and proportions, and to mis-understand the decoration. The coarse and clumsy versions in which much of their work consisted combine the incompetent with the grotesque. The best and earliest Pontic ware was per-haps produced by Greek or Greek-trained craftsmen. Its in-spiration is to be found in a group of amphoras, found chiefly in the west, which are products of an Athenian workshop but in a style uncharacteristic of Athens at the time (575–50 B.C.). These 'Tyrrhenian' amphoras look like the fruits of an effort to break into a market controlled by the popularity of the Corinthian animal-frieze decoration.

CHALCIDIAN

It has been much discussed whether so-called 'Chalcidian' ware was of Euboean manufacture, exported to and popular in the west, or whether it was indeed made in a Chalcidian colony, probably Rhegium. Like the 'Tyrrhenian' amphoras, it is a ware made for a western market. Corinthian influences discernible here too may be attributed to their current favour in the west, but there are Attic and perhaps Ionic elements in it also, combining to produce what has been described as 'prob-ably the most satisfactory decorative pottery of the sixth century'. It too had an animal style, but the figure-scenes on the best examples, among which amphoras, hydrias, cups and kraters predominate, are well designed and make pleasing and effective compositions.

CAERETAN HYDRIAS

If the 'Chalcidian' painters were Euboean expatriates, farther north there were, as it seems, two Greek, perhaps Ionian, emigrants who settled at Etruscan Caere and there produced a series of some thirty hydrias of the first quality. That illustrated is perhaps the earliest of them (*c.* 530 B.C.), and they cover a period of twenty to thirty years. These two, the 'Knee-painter' and the 'Busiris-painter', follow the Tyrrhenian and Pontic preference for horizontal zones of decoration, but they almost always keep their figure-scenes for the handle-zone and use vegetable or other decorative patterns for the remainder. The colour of the clay, generally a warm and cheerful brown, combines with the uninhibited use of added purple and white to produce one of the most enjoyable of all Greek pottery styles.

Plate 71

SOUTH ITALIAN SCHOOLS

At about the time of the foundation of Thurii, perhaps not unconnected with it, two schools of vase-painting based on contemporary Attic grew up in the Taras region of southern Italy, and a third began almost simultaneously in Campania. This last, known as the 'Owl-Pillar Group' from the motif of two of the best-known of the sixty-odd pieces, offered poor imitations of Attic vases of the time and rapidly died out. The former, on the other hand, had important consequences, for they stimulated a local manufacture which blossomed, in the early fourth century, into the great schools of south Italian vase-painting. Some of the early Italiot work is as good as the best Attic. But the western artists found stylistic restraint irksome, and they preferred, and executed with verve and ingenuity, the more baroque effects which achieved popularity at the close of the fifth century.

LUCANIAN

Two of these schools, the Apulian and Lucanian, have only recently become the subject of more intensive study, and now that the archaic and classical pottery styles of the Aegean have been fairly exhaustively treated they may begin to offer the student of vase-painting an attraction they have failed to exercise hitherto. The best of the work, especially in the early stages, is competent and effective. The worst of the developed style lapses into the barbaric, as non-Greek imitators strove to reproduce ideas they could not share. The bell-krater was a favoured vase-type, and the Lucanian potters, deriving their style from Group A of the early south-Italian period, tended to decorate these with two- or three-figure groups—often consisting of static young men or not-so-static satyrs and bacchantes. Yet the work of the Pisticci and Amykos painters, who were their fifth-century ancestors, makes of the same groupings compositions of a pleasantly innocuous kind. Later, the style became florid and its motifs meaningless, and the school seems not to have outlived the fourth century.

APULIAN

Apulian, which lasted just about as long, is somewhat better. Here again the bell-krater was particularly favoured, and on these and other large vases the Apulian painters composed, in a rather stilted manner, statuesque figure-scenes, often in two superposed friezes, which quickly lapse into dullness. Of the Sisyphus-painter, named from a fine volute-krater in Munich showing the wedding of Sisyphus, twenty-one works have been identified, and these and other vases by painters under his influence represent the best of this school (late fifth century). Their successors have been divided into 'the ornate and the ordinary' neither group having much to offer artistically, though the lavish use of added colour by the former makes their often overloaded ornamentation sometimes rather attractive.

Plates 68, 69

CAMPANIAN

In Campania the fourth century saw a school of vase-painting which owed much to Apulian, though its standards were a good deal inferior. Surprisingly, it found a market in eastern Sicily and had some effect on later fourth-century vase-painting there. One of the best Campanian pieces is a calyx-krater in Oxford (*c.* 350–25 B.C.) by the Lloyd-painter, depicting the frolics of some satyrs and maenads. Like Apulian, Campanian came to favour a decoration of female heads framed in luxuriant vegetable motifs.

PAESTAN

Though developed from the Campanian, the Paestan school was superior to it in style and artistry. Posidonia, while under Lucanian political domination, retained much of its Hellenic character, and Greek mythological scenes were popular on the best vases of this group, which began with the Dirce-painter (375–50 B.C.). The masters of the Paestan school in the next generation were Asteas and Python, their names known from signed pieces. Asteas' work has a monumental quality which in lesser hands becomes merely heavy: it appears to excellent effect on two vases found by Sestieri in 1957 and now in the Paestum museum, a lekythos showing Orestes' purification at Delphi and a cup with a seated woman flanked by an eros and a serving-girl; the amount of white in the latter composition is unusual but attractive. Python was less accomplished and owed much to Asteas. The piece illustrated is his best-known one, but a comparison between the 'Odysseus and the Sirens' of his bell-krater in Berlin and the version of the same scene by the Attic Siren-painter is indicative of the loss of vitality which the vase-painter's art has undergone. This south Italian red-figure painting also produced an interest in monumental painting among the local Italians. Known from polychrome frescoes painted on the walls of tombs, the earliest and most Greek in style shows a series of dancing girls from a tomb at Ruvo, now in the Naples museum (later fifth century). Later paintings from Paestum and Cumae evidence the same infusion of the Italic into the Hellenic noted in the vase-series.

Plate 70

Fig. 3

PHLYAX-VASES

The south Italians developed a fondness for pictures drawn from the comic stage, and the vases so decorated are known as *phlyax*-vases. Some one hundred and fifty in number, they are mostly Apulian in origin, though about one-fifth are of the Paestan school. The stubby, grimacing figures, often burlesquing some mythological scene, have a cheerful and friendly appeal which relieves the tedium of much of the more pretentious 'fine-style' contemporary with them. They are by no means the products of lesser artists; both Asteas and Python painted phlyax-scenes, Asteas' best being a bell-krater in Berlin showing a miser and his treasure-chest the victims of a couple of robbers. The Odysseus here illustrated is a refreshing parody of the Siren-painter's grim hero.

Fig. 23

CENTURIPAE WARE

It remains to add a brief mention of a class of polychrome vases, with matt-painting and added plastic ornament, which originate from Centuripae. Probably dateable to the early Hellenistic period, the main types are large kraters and conical dishes with lids, and among the range of colours red and blue, delicately pale on most of the preserved examples,predominate. This ware, quite unlike anything that preceded it, is an interesting phenomenon of the Siculo-Greek culture which the centuries of amalgamation had by then produced.

Plate 73

SCULPTURE AND RELATED ARTS

This is a wide category, and the western achievement within it was somewhat uneven. In monumental sculpture, whether free-standing or as part of a building, the Western Greeks had little to offer that was impressive; but in terracotta they produced statuary of a high order, both large- and small-scale, and revetments for their archaic sanctuaries of a quality which has already been discussed. The artistry of their best terracotta figurines was matched by that of their bronzes, while in the art of engraving coin-dies they were scarcely excelled in the whole of antiquity. In the short compass of this section little can be said to substantiate these generalisations, but with them in mind the reader who visits the museums of Sicily and Magna Graecia, or studies at his leisure the growing range of high-quality illustrations, will perhaps substantiate them from his own experience.

The great sculptors lived in Aegean Greece, and it was there

SCULPTURE IN BRONZE AND STONE

that the finest work in the archaic and classical periods was done. But the west, was, nevertheless, the home of a few artists whose reputation was international. Most famous of these was Pythagoras, originally of Samos, who settled in Rhegium but whose services were commissioned for dedications at Olympia and Delphi. A bronze Europa-and-bull group of his at Taras was a particularly fine piece of work, but for us his style may be best appreciated in the 'Omphalos Apollo' (National Museum, Athens), an unexciting and conservative figure which has been associated with him. The Rhegine, Clearchus, said to have been his teacher, was well enough known to make a bronze Zeus for the Spartans; Dameas and Patrocles of Croton are also named as having made statues to local order for dedication at Olympia.

Plate 60

Of the few monumental stone or bronze figures of the archaic period that survive in the west, the *kouros* from Megara Hyblaea (mid-sixth century) is perhaps the finest, but does not match its Aegean contemporaries in understanding or technique. Later in date (*c.* 500) and more skilfully executed is a near-classical *kouros* from Leontini, also in Syracuse. A head in Catania, perhaps to be associated with it, is reminiscent of the Strangford Apollo. Another *kouros* of the same period in Syracuse wears a cloak, which is in any case unusual and in this case inelegant; a similar provincialism is maintained in a youth of *c.* 460 from Selinus, now at Castelvetrano. Sculpturally the west remained a decade or two behind the times. Yet the Piombino Apollo, apparently from southern Italy, is a heavily built but not ungraceful youth, and a seated goddess from Taras, now in Berlin, a figure some five feet high, has a kind of old-fashioned dignity and is the work of a competent if scarcely *avant-garde* south Italian. The 'Delphic Charioteer' is also a not undistinguished western contribution to the greatest of Greek sanctuaries. A generation later, the head of Apollo from the Crimisa temple is a western version of the 'Phidian' style, and the Boston and

Ludovisi 'thrones' reflect both the excellences and the limitations of western sculptural technique.

Architectural sculptures show a self-confident perkiness which one may believe characteristic of the west. The lively series of metopes from Treasury I and the temple at Foce del Sele have vigorous charm, although the dancing maidens are not the equal of their sisters on a terracotta relief from Rhegium now in the Reggio museum. The classical metopes from Temple E at Selinus are fine pieces and justly celebrated, but seem remote from the best contemporary work in Greece, for example at Olympia, and despite a busy century of temple-building the west appears not to have explored this artistic line of development further. The reliefs for which Taras came to be notable are not apparently related to building construction.

Plate 62

TERRACOTTAS

Western sites have proved extremely rich in terracotta dedications, particularly in small head-and-shoulders or whole-figure images of Hera, Demeter and Persephone, whose cults were evidently very popular. Most collections in the area have a wide range in date and type, some examples being rough and poor in execution and others showing remarkable artistic gifts and a thorough mastery of plastic technique. Important centres of terracotta production appear to have been Gela, Taras and Posidonia. At the last-named the 1952 excavations yielded a long series of fine dedications to Hera, and this site is also notable for the so-called 'donne fiore'—heads which blossom into a flower at the top and were used perhaps for burning incense. Seated or standing female figures, often holding a pig or a dove, are the most regular of the Hera-types, but almost the entire pantheon is represented among the surviving finds. In the Hellenistic period female figurines, draped or undraped, of the more elongated 'Lysippan' proportions were particularly favoured, along with erotes and grotesque, perhaps theatrical, figures of the type found in local vase-painting. Small terracotta altars often carry well-executed reliefs. One of the best,

Plate 72 from Heraclea Minoa, is in Agrigento, but good examples are also to be found in particular at Gela, Syracuse and Reggio.

Plate 79 The early fifth-century series of *pinakes* from Locri, of exquisite workmanship and charming design, has already been mentioned: similar votive plaques from Taras should also be cited. The horseman in Reggio and his companion-piece in the Naples museum are not the sole representatives of monumental terracotta statuary in the west. An archaic Zeus and the remains of antefixes in the form of life-size female *protomae* illustrate the quality of such work at Posidonia, while a seated Demeter or Persephone, found near Grammichele, and a horseman-akroterion from Camarina may reflect Sicilian competence in the same field. The great architectural fragments in terracotta, of which the flying Gorgon from Syracuse may stand as an example, need to be seen in their full and effective colours. Design and execution, always competent, was often masterly. It seems that in this field the Western Greeks made up for their relative lack of ability and originality in stone and that, being fortunate in the substantial remains they have succeeded in leaving behind, they have been able to show off their talents to better advantage.

Plate 22

Plate 78

Fig. 24. Handle of bronze mirror from tomb 749, Locri, now in the Museo Archeologico, Reggio di Calabria: 37.1 cm. high, it is the largest found in the necropolis. Not later than the fifth century B.C.

SMALL BRONZES

Figurines in bronze, whether free-standing or as part of a vase or other article of use, show a liveliness and quality which suggest that the bronze-workers of the west were artists of skill and imagination, with comparatively little of the provincial about them. The great krater of Vix may be Tarentine, and if so its execution, in the *ensemble* and in detail, is silently eloquent of the accomplishment of its makers. Lions were a regular feature as a motif on the handles of bronze vases, and may be seen at their best on several of the eight vases (of *c.* 530 B.C.) found filled with honey in the sealed underground 'sanctuary of the Nymph' at Posidonia. One engagingly rears his neck over the vase's rim and appears to drink from its contents. A similar though less well-preserved hydria found between Gela and Licata illustrates the beauty of form and line achieved in these western bronzes.

Plates 31–33

Plate 76

Work of the archaic and classical periods was often most effective in the miniature. A little lion from Locri is probably part of a lost vase, and while many examples of human figures could deservedly claim illustration a fifth-century girl, also in the Reggio museum, is an especially charming example. Among household utensils other than vases, such as dishes, lamps, mirrors and so forth, a large *candelabrum* from the Locri cemetery, a kind of tree supported by a *kouros* and ending with an elegant *kore* at the top, is an unusual and striking piece.

Plate 75

Plate 74

Fig. 24

Fig. 25

Fig. 26

COINAGE: THE ARTISTS

It remains to consider the coinage of the Western Greeks in its artistic context. Here again such illustrations as have been included in this book will, it is to be hoped, give an impression of the high quality and charm of their achievement and an encouragement to see more of it. The types are varied and fascinating, seldom dull, often ingenious, at times superb, and offer a source of artistic pleasure unsuspected by some and readily appreciated by all. Unusually, the names of the artists are in one or two cases known, for the designers of the great Syracusan, Catanaean and Acragantine coinage of the late fifth and early fourth centuries incorporated their signatures. Cimon and Evaenetus (perhaps Athenians by birth and training), Myron, Polycrates and Euclidas stand out as artists of the highest rank in any company. Earlier in the fifth century, coins of Aetna, Catana and Naxos were designed by an anonymous artist whose gifts, traceable in his consistent style, have earned him the name of the Aetna Master. The Dionysus and Silenus of his Naxian tetradrachma are perhaps his finest achievement. The Syracusan Demareteion, also the work of an anonymous master, couples skilful use of the design-field with a beauty and grace which, although achieved within a diameter of $1\frac{1}{2}$ inches, photographic enlargement can only enhance.

Plates 42*b*, 80

Plate 61*b*

The early coinage of some south Italian cities is remarkable in that the reverses, instead of showing a different image, are incuse reproductions of the relief on the obverse. The city-emblems —the striding Poseidon of Posidonia, the barley-ear of Metapontum, the bull of Sybaris, for instance—are all neatly executed and compare favourably with contemporary coins in the Aegean. The coinage of Sicily similarly showed city-badges, usually paired in the archaic period with a geometrical device. The cock of Himera, dolphin of Zancle, eagle and crab of Acragas all make their appearance in the later sixth century as

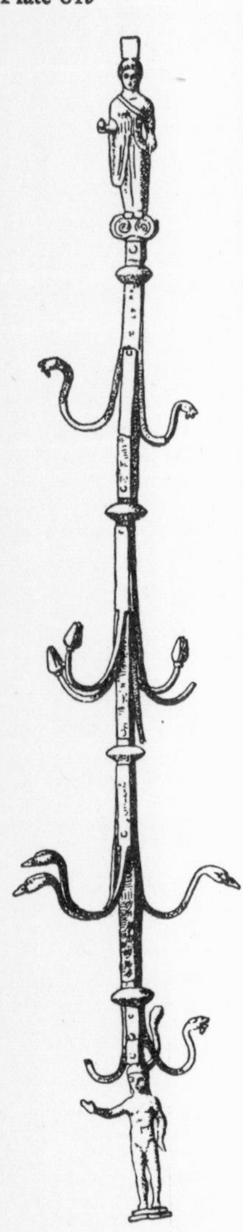

Fig. 25. (left) Sixth-century candelabrum of bronze and iron from tomb 739, Locri, now in the Museo Archeologica, Reggio: it is 1.225 m. high. At its discovery the hand of the skeleton in the tomb was grasping it.

Fig. 26. (right) Bronze kouros and kore: two details from the candelabrum of Fig. 25

forerunners of later and more sophisticated versions, while the device of Gela, a man-headed bull, is seen on a particularly notable issue of the early fifth century. In antiquity coins were useful vehicles of political propaganda. Theron's union of Acragas and Himera is an example in point, for it is numismatically illustrated by an issue combining the cock and the crab on a single coin.

Plate 61a

Later coin-series show the general characteristics of Hellenistic art in their virtuosity. Issues of Syracuse under Timoleon make use of Corinthian types to stress the Syracusan debt to their metropolis. Agathocles at first used similar types but later, as king, adopted various designs, his tetradrachmas showing on the reverse a head of Persephone in the Evaenetus tradition. The coins of Hieron II offer a revealing portrait of one of the most enlightened of the Syracusan autocrats. But these later designers, though efficient, had little to say that was not being better said elsewhere, and it is on the earlier coinage that the justifiable western claim to pre-eminence in die-engraving must depend.

Plate 55a

Fig. 15

PHILOSOPHY, SCIENCE AND RHETORIC

In the maturing city-state of the sixth century B.C., the ferment of ideas which developed so many aspects of the Greek genius also produced the first scientific enquiries into the nature of the physical world and man's place in it. These, though initially concentrated among the Eastern Greeks, with the philosophers of Miletus particularly fertile in theory and counter-theory, did not leave the Greeks in the west unaffected. About 530 B.C. the Samian Pythagoras migrated to Croton, then on the threshold of its finest period, where he expounded a philosophy combining the new physics with the need for a religious hypothesis and with the problem of man in society. His 'way of life' gave a religious connotation to a theory of the world based on numerical analysis, and among his followers he established

PYTHAGORAS

a code of conduct founded on a certain asceticism and a strict personal discipline. Of the practical results of his teaching in the political life of Croton something has already been said. His fame became legendary, and because he left nothing in writing it is hard to distinguish fact from fiction about him. His great learning and the force of his personality are, however, well attested. The well-known Euclidean 'theorem' (which may indeed be his) hardly requires comment. His numerical theory is known to have attached particular religious importance to the number 10, expressed as an equilateral triangle of units formed by the first four integers, and he evolved from this number-mysticism a view of the universe as constructed according to laws of mathematical proportion, expressed as an identification of physical things with numbers. The soul was a divine spark imprisoned in human or animal bodies for a cycle of existences, which might be shortened by strict adherence to the rules of the Pythagorean life, especially to a vegetarianism imposed by the doctrine that all life was akin.

ALCMAEON

Of his followers in the next generation the Crotoniate Alcmaeon was the most distinguished; he was particularly interested in bodily health as the expression of Pythagorean balance and proportion. Later in the fifth century the Pythagorean Philolaus, also of Croton, is credited with a cosmology in which both earth and sun revolve round a central fire. Pythagoras' mathematics reached their zenith in the studies of Archytas, a friend of Plato and for many years a leading statesman in Taras, who was concerned with the ratios of musical intervals as well as with problems of geometry and mechanics.

PHILOLAUS

ARCHYTAS

The influence of Pythagoras in Magna Graecia was far-reaching and long-lasting, but it was sharply distinguished from currents of thought elsewhere in the west. The Phocaean colony at Elea produced two of the most notable of Greek thinkers, the first of whom, Parmenides, brought earlier theories

PARMENIDES

of the nature of matter to a logical *impasse* from which later philosophers could extricate themselves only with serious difficulty. 'What is, is; what is not, is not and cannot be,' was a line of thought which denied empty space and reduced all being to a material, static, spherical, unchangeable and continuous *plenum*. This Parmenides set out in a poem, some fragments of which survive; in it the 'way of truth'—that which *is*—was set over against the 'way of appearance', in which opposites do seem to exist—that is, our apprehension of the physical world, which he dismisses as utterly false. With him for the first time the judgement of reason and that of the senses are brought into sharp contrast, with credit given only to the former.

XENOPHANES

Born about 515 B.C., Parmenides visited Athens about 450 and there met the young Socrates. In a dialogue named after him Plato used his doctrines as a starting-point for a critique of his own theory of forms. He is sometimes alleged to have been influenced by Xenophanes, of Ionian Colophon, who as a young man migrated to the west (*c.* 545 B.C.). It is true that Xenophanes paved the way for a stricter conception of unity and is notable for his thoroughgoing rejection of popular polytheism and for the remarkable doctrine of one god, without human form and motionless himself, governing the movements of the universe by thought alone; but to call him the founder of the Eleatic school is an exaggeration.

ZENO

Zeno of Elea (born *c.* 490) was Parmenides' pupil and accompanied him on his Athenian visit. He defended his position against the criticism of opponents by demonstrating the logical impossibility of a contrary view. 'If there is a multiplicity of being, things will be both infinitely large and infinitely small; and the things that are will be infinite.' Not only must plurality be denied, but motion also. The paradoxes of Achilles and the tortoise, and of the flying arrow, dealt with the latter. Achilles can never overtake the tortoise, since whenever he reaches the point where the tortoise *was*, the tortoise has moved forward—a process which continues even to the smallest subdivisions of the distance between them. The arrow is, at any given point of time, occupying an area equal to its own dimensions; it is thus never to be conceived as in motion, but as being always in a succession of states of rest. Zeno's arguments were skilfully propounded, and he is said by Aristotle to have discovered the technique of dialectic. The association of Elea with this type of philosophical exposition is further illustrated by Plato's introduction of an 'Eleatic stranger' into his dialogues *Sophistes* and *Politicus*.

EMPEDOCLES In attributing dialectic to Zeno, Aristotle at the same time speaks of Empedocles as the 'discoverer' of rhetoric. As with Pythagoras, so many stories grew up around this greatest of the citizens of Acragas that it is hard to discern the real figure behind them. The peak of his career seems to have fallen *c.* 450–40 B.C., in the period immediately following the emancipation of Acragas from the Emmenid tyranny, and he apparently took a prominent part in politics as a champion of the new democracy, breaking up an oligarchic clique and refusing autocratic power when he might have achieved it. His two poems, 'On Nature' and 'Purifications', have seemed to many scholars to offer contradictory views on existence, the former presenting a physical interpretation of all matter and the second showing more reliance on Pythagorean transmigration of souls. While Empedocles agreed with Parmenides that what is is, and is everywhere, he postulated a plurality of elements which are. These—earth, air, fire and water—have the attributes of Parmenides' 'one' and give rise to all kinds of compounds; in their compound state they are apprehensible by the senses, which are in consequence relatively reliable guides. But compounds are not automatic creations. They are produced by the operation of 'love' and 'hate', forces which propel or repel and which in a cosmic context produce cycles of integration and disintegration. The story of Empedocles' suicide on Mount Etna by disappearing into the crater in the hope of being thought to have become a god must regretfully be set aside as legend. Nothing in fact is known of the manner or date of his death.

GORGIAS

His connexion with rhetoric joins him at once with Gorgias of Leontini, whose professional career of philosophic teaching sets him among the group of late-fifth-century professors designated 'sophists'. Born about 483 B.C., he lived on into the fourth century, and the complex style of his oratory, which so enthralled the Athenians during his visit in 427, had a great effect on the prose of his time—as the speeches in Thucydides' *History* illustrate. Plato regarded training in the persuasive art of rhetoric as dangerous when given (or sold) to students insufficiently wise to use it properly, and in his *Gorgias* the old professor appears as a rather naïve figure: but this did him an injustice. The art of speaking formed only one of his interests. He too wrote 'On Nature' (subtitled 'On Non-Existence'), maintaining in satirical contrast to Parmenides that 'nothing is'. What is more, even if anything does exist we cannot know it, and even if we knew it we could not communicate our knowledge.

OTHER RHETORICIANS

The development of rhetoric was a distinctively western contribution to the life of the city-state. Earlier than Gorgias come the shadowy figures of Corax and Teisias, both Syracusans of the post-Deinomenid period who wrote treatises on the subject. Of that of Teisias, pupil of Corax and also teacher of Gorgias, some fragments, too inconsiderable to be informative about their author, perhaps survive in a papyrus from Egyptian Oxyrhynchus. Younger than Gorgias, and severely handled by Socrates in Plato's *Gorgias*, was the Acragantine teacher of rhetoric Polus, whose oratory, if accurately reflected by Plato in a passage set in his mouth, was of an exaggerated and overstrained type.

THE LATER PERIOD

In the fourth and later centuries Sicily and Italy were scarcely fertile ground for philosophic study, and in any case, as Athens established itself as the Mecca of philosophers, independent 'local' schools of thought tended to disappear. Plato came to Syracuse in the hope of testing in practice some of his political theory, but his experiences were discouraging. Dionysius II was neither of age nor of character to be good material for him to work on. Thus neither in philosophic 'research' nor in practical application could the west add further to the history of classical Greek thought. It was in mathematics that, with Archimedes, its greatest contribution was yet to be made. Archimedes' best-known discoveries concern mechanics—not only his engines of war but his invention of the 'Archimedean' screw and his treatises on levers and the balance and movement of heavy weights. But his geometrical studies gave him the greater claim to fame, and his approximate computation of the value of π by an arithmetical study was a remarkable *tour de force*. The complexity of his work became proverbial, and he himself reckoned as his greatest discovery the ratio (3 : 2) between a cylinder and a sphere circumscribed by it, for we are told that this was, by his instructions, represented on his tomb. His death, in the confusion of Marcellus' capture of Syracuse, fittingly symbolises the extinction of independent Greek scientific development in the west.

ARCHIMEDES

Chapter VI

Envoi

The three preceding chapters have dealt in turn with the establishment by the Greeks of new settlements in the western Mediterranean, with the fortunes that befell them, and with the part they played in the development of Hellenic culture. The treatment has been summary, but whatever the length of such a discussion one ultimate question must arise: what is our assessment of the Western Greeks' place in the Greek achievement? 'Hellenism' as the sum total of that achievement is and always has been a positive force, though few would reckon to make a satisfactory definition of it. It has its subjective and objective aspects: that is, while Greek attainment in this or that significant instance may be objectively noted, it will be of a deeper significance for some than for others. The Hellenic legacy exists for all the world; yet we are all independent beneficiaries, to the extent that we care to grasp and appreciate the heritage.

The hope is that this book has not only led up to this ultimate question but has also made its reader anxious to face and answer it for himself; for all such answers must be personal—*quot homines*, perhaps, *tot sententiae*. In answering, however, three considerations at least ought not to be left out of account. The first is that the total legacy of Hellas is unthinkable without the west. Its contribution of men and monuments, art, thought and deeds is too great to be overlooked, too integral to every aspect of Greek studies to be put aside into a separate compartment. Secondly, there is the transmission of Hellenism to western posterity, through Rome. Horace's familiar tag, that captive Greece took captive her fierce conqueror, is only half true; the

Western Greeks had already done it. Their alphabet had long since reached Rome; Greek epic, Greek tragedy and Greek comedy had been translated into Roman terms before one Roman soldier set foot in Greece; Greek thought, Greek political practice, architectural and artistic canons were already known to and impressing themselves on a Rome only too eager to absorb them. This mediation of Greece to Rome, embodied so vividly for us in the remains of Pompeii, puts us greatly ni the debt of the western colonists, whose initial work it was.

The Greek genius, thus transmitted, has its meaning for us. Not because we learn from Greek history or profit by examples of Greek virtues and vices: such a utilitarian view cannot well be maintained in any case, and would be applicable to any historical period and people if it could. The principles of western culture and the premisses of western thought rest on foundations which the Greeks laid, and the quality of their achievements offers, as it has always offered, a permanent enrichment to all who seek it—the more thorough the quest the greater the reward. Here, for the opportunity of searching and for the value of the prize, we may be allowed to record some particular gratitude to the Greeks in the west.

Glossary

Some readers may welcome a note or two in explanation of a few technical words which have been introduced into the text of this book, and the following may perhaps prove helpful:

Abacus. In the Greek orders of architecture, the upper section of a capital, rectangular in the Doric order.
Akroterion. Sculptured decoration in terracotta or stone, sometimes a human figure or an equestrian group, set on a plinth above the corner or apex of a pediment.
Agora. In a Greek city, an open area serving as market- or meeting-place, much as a modern Italian piazza.
Antefix. A decorative facing on the end of the lowest tile of the ridge of cover-tiles masking the junction between the flat pantiles of a roof.
Architrave. In the Greek orders of architecture, the course of beams or stone blocks immediately above the columns.
Aryballos. In Corinthian pottery, a small round or ovoid flask with a narrow neck.
Cavea. The auditorium of a Greek theatre, customarily built into a hill-side.
Cella. The principal interior room of a Greek temple. Where a smaller room exists beyond and opening out of the cella, it is known as an *adyton*.
Echinus. In a Doric capital, the convex member between the column-shaft and the abacus.
Entasis. The convex curve of the shaft of a column.
Hoplite. The heavy-armed foot-soldier of the Greek city-state army. The citizen-soldier provided his own equipment, and in consequence his enrolment in the hoplite ranks depended on his possession of a qualifying amount of property (the *hoplite-census*).
Isodomic masonry. Masonry in which the courses are of equal height.
Kouros. Statue of a standing male figure, always youthful and usually nude, in a frontal pose with one leg advanced. The term is particularly associated with the archaic period of Greek sculpture.

Krater. A large, deep bowl on a wide foot, chiefly used for mixing wine.
Lekythos. In its sixth–fifth-century form, a small vase used as an oil-flask, oval in shape with a rather narrow body and an angled shoulder, above which a slender neck is terminated in a strong, thick lip. The body stands on a small base.
Metope. A panel, often decorated with painting or sculpture, between two triglyphs of a Doric building, in the course above the architrave (the *frieze*).
Opisthodomos. A false porch at the back of a temple, open to the peristyle but usually not communicating with the *cella* or *adyton.*
Palaestra. A building or complex of buildings for athletic training and exercise.
Pediment. The triangular area at either end of the ridge roof of a Greek building, above the horizontal cornice.
Peristyle. A covered colonnade surrounding a building. A temple so surrounded is said to be *peripteral.*
Prostyle. A temple so described has a row of columns, other than those of a peristyle, in front of its main door.
Regula. In the Doric order, a narrow strip projecting below the broad flat moulding (*taenia*) at the top of the architrave, and recurring below each triglyph. Below the regulae project the *guttae,* carved in the shape of cylindrical pegs.
Stoa. A portico, often of considerable length, closed at the back and with a row of columns on the open long side. In larger examples there may be one or two interior rows of columns, and the closed long side may accommodate shops.
Triglyph. In the frieze of a Doric building, an element projecting between the metopes and carved with two vertical channels; the edges towards the metopes are chamfered.
Tyrant. The absolute ruler of a Greek city-state, who achieves or maintains his position without a constitutional basis, often as the result of revolution. The word does not necessarily connote savagery or misuse of autocratic power.

Select Bibliography

The literature on the various subjects covered by this book is voluminous. I have selected principally those books and articles which I have found especially helpful and interesting, those which give the general reader a clear and authoritative summary of a particular site or subject, and those which may be regarded as 'standard' studies. These three categories are by no means mutually exclusive; many an entry qualified under all three heads. In any case, the selection involved makes such a bibliography as this into rather a subjective affair, and I have not attempted to fill every gap. Chapter III presents a special bibliographic problem, which is discussed below.

GENERAL

E. A. Freeman, *History of Sicily* (1891–4).
A. Holm, *Geschichte Siziliens* (1870–98).
B. Pace, *Arte e Civiltà della Sicilia antica* (1935–49).
E. Pais, *Storia della Sicilia e della Magna Graecia* (1894).
D. Randall-MacIver, *Greek Cities in Italy and Sicily* (1931).
I. Scaturro, *Storia di Sicilia—l'età antica* (1950).

(Volumes of good illustrations):
L. Bernabò Brea, *Musei e Monumenti in Sicilia* (1958).
L. von Matt (text by P. Griffo), *Das Antike Sizilien* (1959) [now also in English and French versions].
H. Schwartz, *Sicily* (1955).

CHAPTER II

L. Bernabò Brea, *Sicily before the Greeks* (1957).
J. Bérard, *La colonisation grecque* (ed. 2, 1957).
G. Pugliese Carratelli, 'Minos e Cocalos', *Kokalos* II, 1956, 89–103.

R. DION, 'Tartessos, l'Océan homérique et les travaux d'Hercule', *Revue Historique* CCXXIV, 1960, 27–44.

T. J. DUNBABIN, 'Minos and Daidalos in Sicily', *Papers of the British School at Rome* (New Series), III, 1948, 1–18.

D. L. PAGE, *The Homeric Odyssey* (1955).

D. L. PAGE, *History and the Homeric Iliad* (1957).

E. D. PHILLIPS, 'Odysseus in Italy', *Journal of Hellenic Studies*, LXXIII, 1953, 53–67.

L. G. POCOCK, *The Sicilian origin of the Odyssey* (1957).

LORD WILLIAM TAYLOUR, *Mycenaean Pottery in Italy and adjacent areas* (1958).

CHAPTER III

The bibliographies provided by J. Bérard, *Bibliographie topographique des principales cités grecques de l'Italie méridionale et de la Sicile dans l'antiquité* (1941), and T. J. Dunbabin, *The Western Greeks* (1948), make it unnecessary to cite earlier material. In the list below, arranged alphabetically by place-name, I have confined the record to publications of 1950 or later, save that, where a site has not been extensively dealt with since then, I have quoted one principal reference of an earlier date.

Accounts of recent archaeological work in 'western Hellas' are given at regular intervals by A. W. van Buren in the *American Journal of Archaeology* and by A. D. Trendall in the *Archaeological Reports* issued under the auspices of the Society for the Promotion of Hellenic Studies. A bibliography to the publication of archaeological material appears annually in the *Fasti Archaeologici*, in the *Bulletin archéologique* included in the *Revue des Études grecques,* and in the *Archäologischer Anzeiger* appended to the *Jahrbuch des Deutschen Archäologischen Instituts.* Full publication of excavations undertaken by the Italian authorities takes place in the *Notizie degli Scavi* or in the *Monumenti Antichi.* A useful account by B. Neutsch of excavations in Sicily during 1949–54 was published in *Archäologischer Anzeiger*, 1954, 465–706.

There is something strange about a bibliography on Western Greek sites which includes the name of Paolo Orsi no more than once. Although, on the principles outlined above, references to his many articles may be sought from Bérard or Dunbabin, it is perhaps in order to take this opportunity of paying tribute to the great work that he did in the field with which we have been dealing.

Acrae, L. Bernabò Brea, *Akrai* (1956).

Acragas, P. Marconi, *Agrigento* (1929).

E. de Miro, 'Il quartiere ellenistico-Romano di Agrigento', *Rendiconti dell'Accademia Nazionale dei Lincei* (Ser. VIII), XII, 1957, 135–40.

(*Monte Saraceno*), D. Adamesteanu, 'Monte Saraceno ed il problema della penetrazione rodiocretese nella Sicilia meridionale', *Archeologia Classica,* VIII, 1956, 121–46.

Crimisa (*Cirò*), P. Orsi, *Templum Apollinis Alaei* (1933).

Cumae, E. Gàbrici, 'Cuma', *Monumenti Antichi,* XXII, 1913.

Elea-Velia, P. Mingazzini, 'Velia', *Atti e Memorie della Società Magna Grecia* (Nuova Serie), I, 1954, 23–60.

P. C. Sestieri, 'Greek Elea—Roman Velia', *Archaeology*, X, 1957, 2–10.

Foce del Sele, P. Zancani Montuoro and U. Zanotti Bianco, *Heraion alla Foce del Sele* (1951–4).

P. Zancani Montuoro, 'Altre Metope scolpite dallo Heraion alla Foce del Sele', *Atti e Memorie della Società Magna Grecia* (N.S.), II, 1958, 9–26.

Gela, D. Adamesteanu and P. Orlandini, *Notizie degli Scavi* (Ser. VIII), X, 1956, 203–401; XIV, 1960, 67–246.

R. van Compernolle, 'Les Deinoménides et le culte de Démèter et Coré à Gela', *Hommages à Waldemar Déonna*, 1957, 474–9.

P. Orlandini, 'Storia e topografia di Gela dal 405 al 282 A.C.', *Kokalos*, II, 1956, 158–76.

(*Butera*), D. Adamesteanu, 'Butera—a Sicilian town through the ages', *Archaeology*, X, 1957, 166–73.

Heraclea Minoa, E. de Miro, *Notizie degli Scavi* (Ser. VIII), XI, 1957, 232–87.

Himera, P. Marconi, *Himera* (1931).

Ischia, G. Buchner, 'Scavi nella necropoli di Pithecusa', *Atti e Memorie della Società Magna Grecia* (N.S.), I, 1954, 11–19.

Locri, A. de Franciscis, 'Ancient Locri', *Archaeology*, XI, 1958, 206–12.

Massalia, F. Villard, *La céramique grecque de Marseille* (1960).

Megara Hyblaea, G. Vallet and F. Villard, 'Les dates de fondation de Megara Hyblaea et de Syracuse', *Bulletin de Correspondance Hellénique*, LXXVI, 1952, 289–346.

G. Vallet and F. Villard: see successive volumes of *Mélanges d'archéologie et d'histoire, École française de Rome* for 1952 and onwards.

Morgantina, see reports published in *American Journal of Archaeology*, LXI, 1957 and succeeding volumes by R. Stillwell and E. Sjöqvist.

Motya, G. A. Ruggieri, 'Motya and Lilybaeum', *Archaeology*, X, 1957, 131–6.

J. I. S. Whitaker, *Motya* (1921).

Posidonia–Paestum, H. Kayser, *Paestum* (1958).

F. Krauss, *Paestum—Die Griechischen Tempel* (1941).

F. Krauss, *Die Tempel von Paestum I—Der Athenatempel* (1959).

F. Krauss and R. Herbig, *Der Korinthische–Dorische Tempel am Forum von Paestum* (1939).

B. Neutsch, Τᾶς Νύνφας ἐμὶ ηιαρόν *zum unterirdischen Heiligtum von Paestum* (1957).

P. C. Sestieri, 'The Antiquities of Paestum', *Archaeology*, VII, 1954, 206–13.

P. C. Sestieri, 'An underground shrine at Paestum', *Archaeology*, IX, 1956, 22–33.

P. C. Sestieri, 'A new painted tomb at Paestum', *Archaeology*, XII, 1959, 33–37.

Rhegium, G. Vallet, *Rhégion et Zancle* (1958).

Segesta, A. M. Burford, 'Temple-building at Segesta', *Classical Quarterly* (New Series), XI, 1961, 87–93.

R. van Compernolle, 'Ségeste et l'Hellénisme', *Phoibos*, V, 1950–1, 183–228.

Selinus, G. Vallet and F. Villard, 'La date de fondation de Sélinonte', *Bulletin de Correspondance Hellénique*, LXXXII, 1958, 16–26.

Sybaris, E. Aletti, *Sibari, Turio, Copia* (1959).

J. S. Callaway, *Sybaris* (1950).

Syracuse, A. Di Vita, 'La penetrazione siracusana nella Sicilia sudorientale', *Kokalos*, II, 1956, 177–205.

M. Guido, *Syracuse* (1958).

Taras, P. Wuilleumier, *Tarente, des origines à la conquête romaine* (1939).

Thurii, see *Sybaris*.

Tyndaris, F. Barreca, 'Tindari colonia Dionigiana', *Rendiconti dell'Accademia Nazionale dei Lincei* (Ser. VIII), XII, 1957, 125–35.
R. R. Holloway, 'Tyndaris, last colony of the Sicilian Greeks', *Archaeology*, XIII, 1960, 246–50.
Zancle-Messana, see *Rhegium*.

See also:

A. R. Burn, *The Lyric Age of Greece* (1960)—esp. 69–89, 143–54.
Rhys Carpenter, 'The Phoenicians in the West', *American Journal of Archaeology*, LXII, 1958, 35–53.
J. L. Myres, *Geographical History in Greek Lands* (1953)—esp. 133–71.

On chapter III section 6 see in particular:

A. R. Burn, *Op. cit.*, 403–8.
R. van Compernolle, A series of articles in *Bulletin de l'Institut historique Belge*, XXVI, 1950–1—XXIX, 1955.
R. M. Cook, *Greek Painted Pottery* (1960), 261–70.
R. M. Cook, 'Ionia and Greece', *Journal of Hellenic Studies*, LXVI, 1946, esp. 70–87.
K. J. Dover, 'La colonizzazione della Sicilia in Tucidide', *Maia*, VI, 1953, 1–20.
T. J. Dunbabin, *The Western Greeks* (1948), Appendix I.
M. T. Piraino, 'Sulla cronologia delle fondazioni siceliote', *Kokalos*, III, 1957, 123–8.
H. Wentker, 'Die Ktisis von Gela bei Thukydides', *Mitteilungen des Deutschen Archäologischen Instituts* (*Roemische Abteilung*), LXIII, 1956, 129–39.

CHAPTER IV

Apart from the standard Histories of Greece, all of which include (as they should and must) an account of the history of the Western Greeks, and in addition to the works listed in the 'General' section above, the following may be found useful:

D. Adamesteanu, 'Osservazioni sulla battaglia die Gela del 405 a.c.', *Kokalos*, II, 1956, 142–57.
H. Berve, *Die Herrschaft des Agathokles* (Sitzungsberichte der Bayerischen Akademie der Wissenschaften, 1952, Heft 5).

H. BERVE, *König Hieron II* (Abhandlungen der Bayerischen Akademie der Wissenschaften, Neue Folge, Heft 47, 1959).

T. J. DUNBABIN, *The Western Greeks* (1948).

P. GREEN, 'The first Sicilian Slave War', *Past and Present*, no. 20, 1961, 10–29.

P. LEVÊQUE, *Pyrrhus* (1957).

G. NENCI, *Pirro* (1953).

ALEXANDER SCHENCK, GRAF VON STAUFFENBERG, *König Hieron II von Syrakus* (1933).

V. M. SCRAMUZZA, *Roman Sicily* (in T. Frank, *An Economic Survey of Ancient Rome*, III, 1937).

K. F. STROHEKER, *Dionysios I* (1957).

H. J. W. TILLYARD, *Agathocles* (1908).

A. VALLONE, 'I Mamertini in Sicilia', *Kokalos*, I, 1955, 22–61.

H. WENTKER, *Sizilien und Athen* (1956).

H. D. WESTLAKE, *Timoleon and his relations with tyrants* (1952).

Volume IV of *Kokalos* (1958) was devoted to a series of articles dealing with Sicily in the time of Timoleon.

CHAPTER V

section 1

V. EHRENBERG, *The Greek State* (1960)—part I.

section 2

F. CASTAGNOLI, *Ippodamo di Mileto* (1956).

A. VON GERKAN, *Griechische Städteanlagen* (1924).

A. KRIESIS, 'Urbanism and Town-Planning', *Acta Congressus Madvigiani*, 1954 (pubd. 1958), IV, 27–86.

R. MARTIN, *L'Urbanisme dans la Grèce antique* (1956).

G. SCHMIEDT and R. CHEVALLIER, *Caulonia e Metaponto* (1959).

R. E. WYCHERLEY, *How the Greeks built cities* (1949)—esp. 15–35.

section 3

The reader will find the principal histories of Greek architecture useful, notably:

W. B. DINSMOOR, *The Architecture of Ancient Greece* (1950).

A. W. LAWRENCE, *Greek Architecture* [Pelican History of Art] (1957).
W. H. PLOMMER, *Ancient and Classical Architecture* (1956).
D. S. ROBERTSON, *Greek and Roman Architecture* (ed. 2, 1943).
And for western architectural detail:
LUCY T. SHOE, *Profiles of Western Greek Mouldings* (1952).

On the theatres see:

M. BIEBER, *A History of the Greek and Roman Theater* (ed. 2, 1961).

For the Tarentine funerary monuments see:

H. KLUMBACH, *Tarentiner Grabkunst* (1937).

For architecture on individual sites see the bibliography to chapter III.

section 4

F. E. ADCOCK, *The Greek and Macedonian Art of War* (1957).
A. W. LAWRENCE, 'Archimedes and the design of Euryalus fort', *Journal of Hellenic Studies,* LXVI, 1946, 99–107.
L. MAUCERI, *Il Castello Eurialo nella storia e nell'arte* (ed. 2, 1939).
H. W. PARKE, *Greek Mercenary Soldiers from the earliest times to the battle of Ipsus* (1933).
R. L. SCRANTON, *Greek Walls* (1941).
W. W. TARN, *Hellenistic military and naval developments* (1930).
R. E. WYCHERLEY, *How the Greeks built cities* (1949)—esp. 36–49.

section 5

J. BOUSQUET, 'Une monnaie d'or de Cyrène sur la côte nord de L'Armorique', *Annales de Bretagne*, LXVIII, 1961, 25–39.
G.-E. BROCHE, *Pythéas le Massaliote* (1936).
M. CARY and E. H. WARMINGTON, *The Ancient Explorers* (1929).
H. J. METTE, *Pytheas von Massalia* (1952).
M. NINCK, *Die Entdeckung von Europa durch die Griechen* (1945)—esp. 179–226.

section 6

C. M. BOWRA, *Greek Lyric Poetry* (ed. 2, 1961).
A. W. PICKARD-CAMBRIDGE, *Dithyramb, Tragedy and Comedy* (1927).
M. PINTO-COLOMBO, *Il Mimo di Sofrone e di Senarcho* (1934).
W. SCHMID and O. STÄHLIN, *Griechische Literaturgeschichte* (1929).

section 7

TRUESDELL S. BROWN, *Timaeus of Tauromenium* (1958).

F. JACOBY, *Fragmente der Griechischen Historiker*, III (1950), section lxix, nos. 554–77.

section 8

J. D. BEAZLEY, 'Groups of Campanian Red-Figure', *Journal of Hellenic Studies*, LXIII, 1943, 66–111.

J. BOARDMAN, 'Early Euboean pottery and history', *Annual of the British School of Archaeology at Athens*, LII, 1957, esp. 12–14.

A. CAMBITOGLOU, 'Groups of Apulian Red-figured vases decorated with heads of women or of Nike', *Journal of Hellenic Studies*, LXXIV, 1954, 111–21.

R. M. COOK, *Greek Painted Pottery* (1960).

J. M. HEMELRIJK, *De Caeretaanse Hydriae* (1956).

G. M. A. RICHTER, *Ancient Italy* (1955)—esp. 1–33.

M. ROBERTSON, *Greek Painting* (1959).

A. D. TRENDALL, *Frühitaliotische Vasen* (1938).

A. D. TRENDALL, *Paestan Pottery* (1936).

A. D. TRENDALL, *Phlyax Vases* (1959).

section 9

Much material relevant to this section is discussed in relation to the place of its discovery, for which see the bibliography to chapter III. I also omit museum catalogues and general works on Greek sculpture, including picture-books of Greek Art which have achieved a wide circulation in recent years.

(*Sculpture*)

B. ASHMOLE, 'Late Archaic and Early Classical Sculpture in Sicily and South Italy' (*Proceedings of the British Academy*, 1934).

A. DE FRANCISCIS, 'Note all'acrolito di Cirò', *Mitteilungen des Deutschen Archäologischen Instituts* (*Römische Abteilung*), LXIII, 1956, 96–101.

P. ORLANDINI, 'Le nuove antefisse Sileniche di Gela e il loro contributo alla conoscenza della coroplastica siceliota', *Archeologia Classica*, VI, 1954, 251–66.

E. Paribeni, 'Di una piccola kore del Museo di Taranto e della scultura in marmo in Magna Grecia', *Atti e Memorie della Società Magna Grecia* (N.S.), I, 1954, 63–70.
G. M. A. Richter, *Ancient Italy* (1955)—esp. 1–33.
P. Zancani Montuoro, 'Note sui soggetti e sulla tecnica delle tabelle di Locri', *Atti e Memorie della Società Magna Grecia* (N.S.), I, 1954, 71–106.

(*Coinage*)

E. Boehringer, *Die Münzen von Syrakus* (1929).
H. A. Cahn, *Die Münzen der Sizilischen Stadt Naxos* (1944).
G. F. Hill, *Coins of Ancient Sicily* (1903).
C. T. Seltman, *Greek Coins* (ed. 2, 1955).
C. T. Seltman, *Masterpieces of Greek Coinage* (1949).
Some of the coins referred to in the text of this section are conveniently illustrated in C. T. Seltman, *A Book of Greek Coins* [King Penguin series] (1952).

section 10

J. Burnet, *Early Greek Philosophy* (ed. 4, 1930).
B. Farrington, *Greek Science* (1944).
W. Jaeger, *The Theology of the early Greek philosophers* (1947).
G. S. Kirk and J. E. Raven, *The Presocratic Philosophers* (1957).

Acknowledgements

A book of this kind relies, directly or indirectly, upon so many people besides its author for its creation that an adequate acknowledgement to all who have in some way contributed to it would be impossible. I am especially grateful to those friends and colleagues who have read some or all of it in manuscript or proof, and whose kindly criticisms have improved or corrected it at many points. In particular Professors W. K. C. Guthrie, Denys L. Page and Homer A. Thompson, Dr Lucy T. Shoe, Dr M. I. Finley, Mr R. M. Cook and Mr G. T. Griffith have readily given me the benefit of their advice and encouragement. I must also record with gratitude my debt to the Travel Fund of the University of Cambridge, and to the Faculty Board of Classics of that University, for generous assistance towards the journeys which form a necessary background to this study.

Many scholars in Italy and Sicily, and the Soprintendenze with which they are concerned, have been generous of their time and good offices in making material available to me and in providing photographs for the plates, the numbers of which I have added to their names. In this connexion particular acknowledgements are due to Professors L. Bernabò Brea and E. de Miro (39, 60, 66, 73, 76), P. Griffo and P. Orlandini (14–16, 46), A. de Franciscis (22, 74–5, 77, 79), M. Napoli (62) and P. C. Sestieri (5), to whom I am also indebted for material on Paestum and Velia. Professor G. Klaffenbach provided the photograph which appears as plate 45, and Professor F. Benoit very kindly supplied plate 30. I acknowledge with gratitude the kindness of Professor R. Joffroy and the Presses Universitaires de France in permitting me to reproduce plates 31–3, and of the Trustees of the British Museum in granting similar permission for plates 29, 38, 42, 55*b*/*c*, 70 and 71. The Master and my colleagues of Corpus Christi College, Cambridge, were kind enough to allow me to reproduce material from the Lewis Collection as plates 68 and 69. Dr Ernest Nash, of the Fototeca di Architettura e Topografia dell'Italia antica, has been consistently helpful, and to his assistance I owe plates 6, 8, 27, 28, 35, 56 and 57. For the print used in plate 7 I am indebted to E.P.T., Messina. Finally, to Mr L. von Matt and NZN-

Buchverlag, Zürich, publishers of *Das Antike Sizilien* (plates 11, 19, 36, 55*a*, 61, 72, 78 and 80), to H. Schwarz and Anton Schroll & Co., Vienna, publishers of *Sicily* (plates 67 and 81), and to Professor M. Hirmer and the Hirmer Verlag, Munich, publishers of *Griechische Tempel und Heiligtümer* (plates 9, 17, 25 and 41), my thanks for permission to make use of their admirable plates. The majority of the illustrations not here accounted for are from my own photographs, and I must thank my wife for her help and patience when they were taken and the staff of the art department of Messrs Thames and Hudson, Ltd, for making the best of them.

Mr H. Shelley redrew the maps, Mr Philip Ward fig. 10, and Mr S. C. Collard many of the other figures. The cast from which fig. 15 was drawn I owe to the Syndics of the Fitzwilliam Museum, Cambridge, and to Mr Graham Pollard.

This is a long list, but it is a pleasure to have the opportunity of recording my sincere gratitude to so many willing helpers for making this book possible—not least to the staff of Messrs Thames and Hudson for unwavering patience and tact from beginning to end.

1

2

3
4

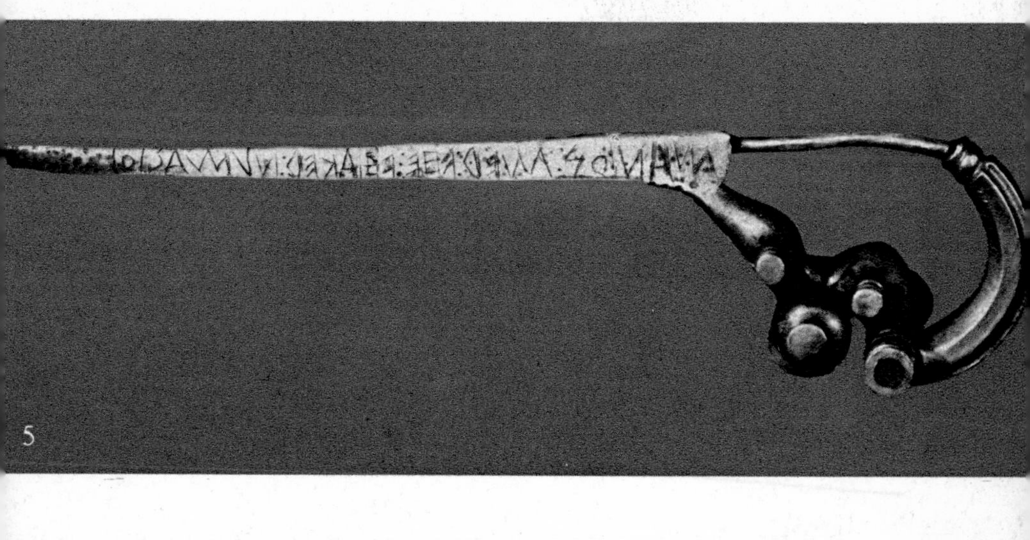
5

6

7

8

9

10

11

15

16

17

18

20

21

23

24

5

6

27

28

29

31

2
3

34

35

37

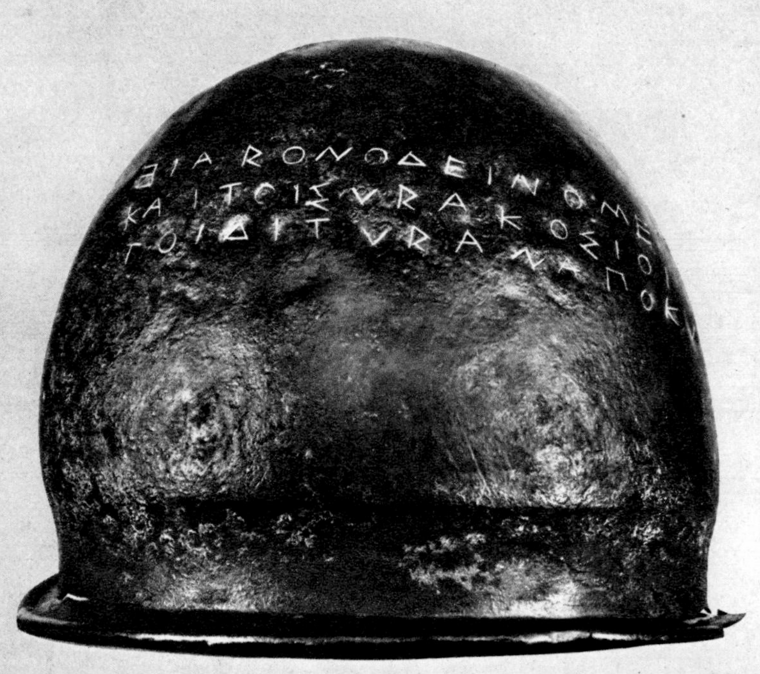

38

39

40

41

42 *a*

42 *b*

43

44

ΛΠ ΘΟΣΡΕΡΙΤ
Ο ΥΜΜΑΧΟΥΣΕΙ
ΥΣΕΚΓΟΝΟΥΣ
Ε ΝΑΕΙΧΡΟΝΟΝ
ΗΝΧΩΡΑΝΤΗΝΑ
Λ ΗΝΗΚΑΤΑΛΘΑΙ
ΚΑΙΤΟΥΣΕΚΓΟΝ
ΛΑΩΣΙΝΑΘΗΝΑ
ΑΤΤΑΝΠΑΝΤ
ΕΑΝΤΙΣΤΗΙΕ
ΣΑΥΤΟΗΟΣΩΗΑ
ΗΚΑΤΑΓΗΝΗΚ
ΡΟΥΣΚΑΘΟΤΙΑ
ΗΚΑΙΚΑΤΑΘΑΛ
Θ ΝΑΤΟΗΟΠΑΛ
Δ ΗΥΣΙΩΙΜΗΔ
Π ΧΩΡΑΝΤΗΝΑ
Κ ΓΗΝΜΗΤΕΚ
Ο ΕΞΕΙΝΑΙΟΠ
Π ΝΜΗΔΕΤΟΥΕΚ

46

47

8

19

50

51

2

53

ΛΙΩΝΙΟΥΛΙΟΝΓΑΙΟΥΥΙΟΝΝΑΣΩΝΑ
ΕΤΗΣΚΑΙΕΥΕΡΓΕΣΙΑΣΕΝΕΚΑ
NATVS ET POPVLVS VELIENSIS
IVLIO C F NASONI HONOR
ET VIRTVTIS CAVSA

4

55 *a* *b* *c*

56

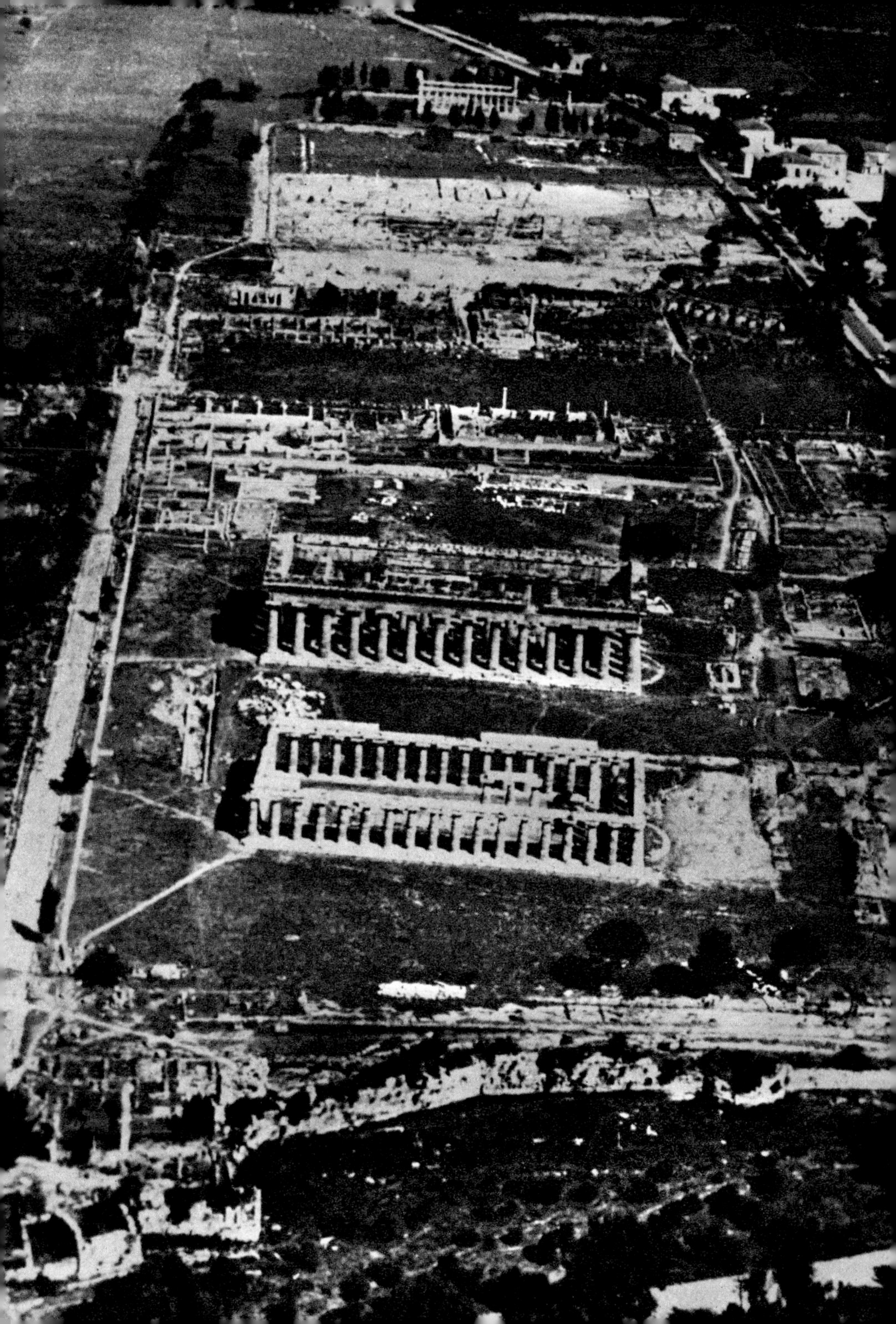

58

59

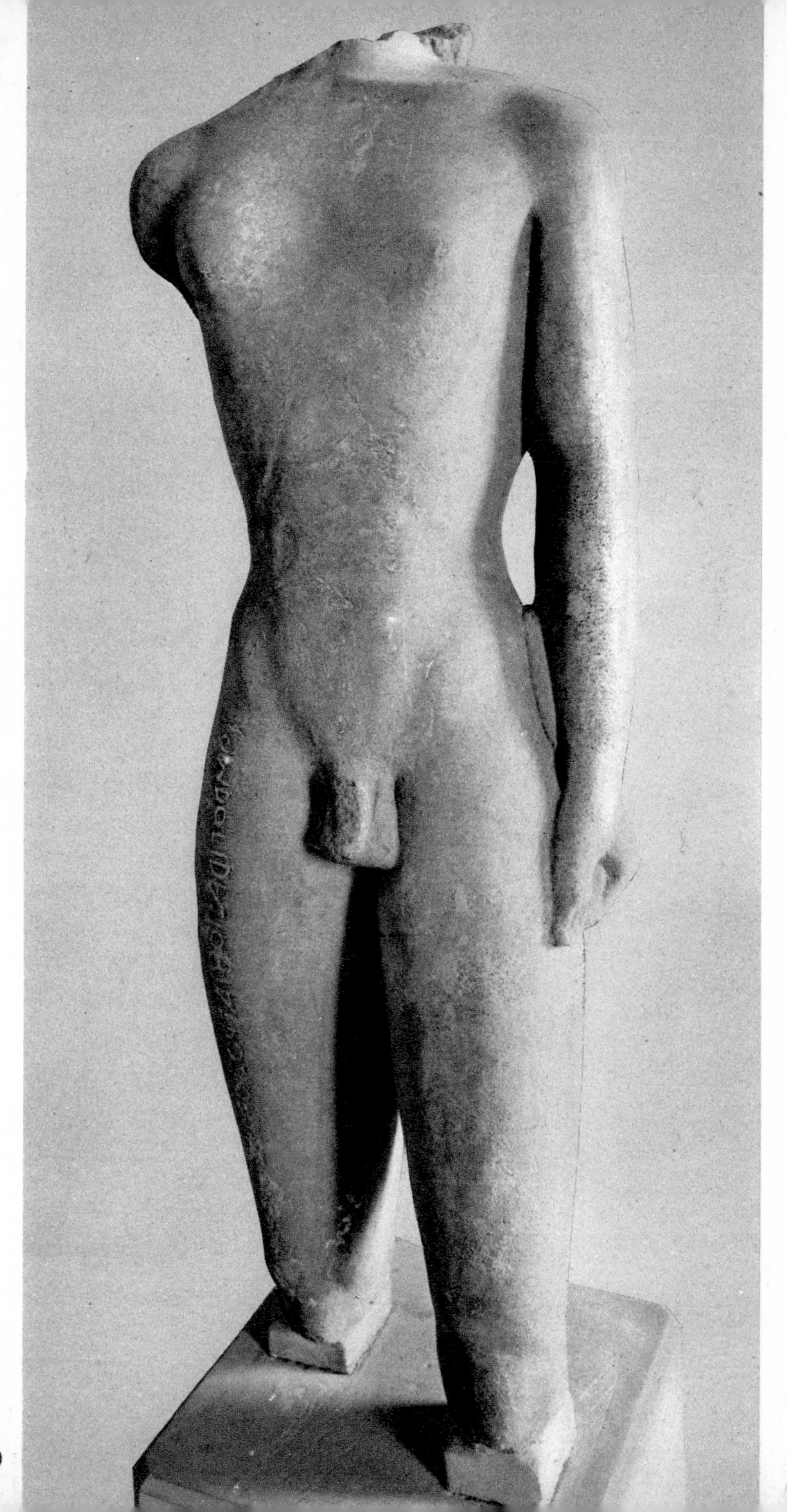

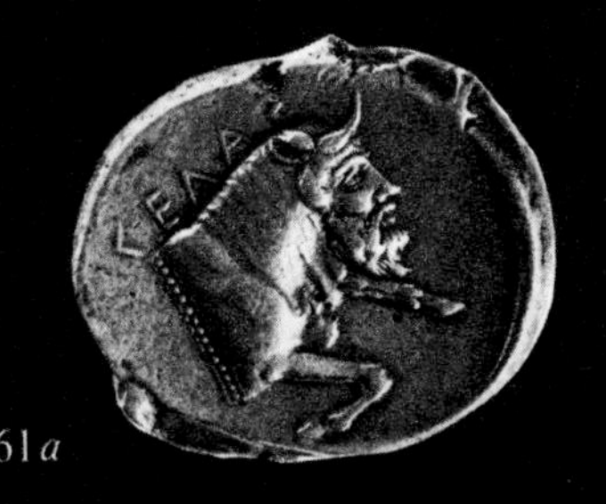

61*a*

61*b*

62

63

64

65

66

67

69

68

71

72

73

74

75

77

78

80

81

Notes on the Plates

1 Bronze dagger discovered in 1845 at Pelynt, Cornwall, which is 'foreign to the British Bronze-Age armoury' and has proved to be of Mycenaean type, attributable to the Myc. III*a* period (fourteenth century B.C.). It is 11 cm. long and 4.7 cm. wide at its widest point. See V. Gordon Childe, *Proceedings of the Prehistoric Society*, XVII, 1951, 95.

2 Part of Stone 53 of the sarsen trilithons of Stonehenge, showing (to the left) a carved dagger of Mycenaean type similar to that of plate 1. It suggests that these daggers were objects familiar to the builders of Stonehenge period III. See J. F. S. Stone, *Wessex before the Celts*, 97–9; R. J. C. Atkinson, *Stonehenge*, 30–1 and plate XIIA.

3 Mycenaean jug found in tomb 37 at Thapsos near Syracuse; 4⅜ in. in height. See L. Bernabò Brea, *Sicily before the Greeks*, plate 60; Lord William Taylour, *Mycenaean pottery in Italy and the adjacent areas*, 59, no. 12 and plate 9, 2.

4 Mycenaean faience beads from the Plemmyrion necropolis south of Syracuse. See L. Bernabò Brea, *op. cit.*, plate 55.

5 Gold *fibula* from Praeneste (Palestrina), said to have come from the Bernardini tomb, and now in the Museo Preistorico-etnografico 'Luigi Pigorini', Rome. It is 11 cm. long, and to be dated to the seventh century B.C. The inscription (retrograde) reads MANIOS MED FHEFHAKED NUMASIOI—'Manius made me for Numerius'. See C. D. Curtis, *Memoirs of the American Academy in Rome*, III, 1919, 21–2, no. 2B; CIL, I^2 ii, 3; CIL, XIV, 4123.

6 The 'Cup of Nestor' from Pithecussae (Ischia). This skyphos, grey-ochre in colour, is 10.3 cm. high and has a maximum diameter of 15.1 cm. It was restored from some fifty small fragments found widely scattered in a cremation tomb (no. 282); the main affinities of its decoration are with Ionia. The incised inscription can be seen in the central fragments

below the plaster restoration. See G. Buchner and C. F. Russo, *Rendiconti della Accademia Nazionale dei Lincei* (Ser. VIII), X, 1955, 215–34.

7 The Bay of Naxos, looking southwards from Taormina. Capo Schisò is the promontory enclosing the bay on the south, and on this the Chalcidian settlers under Thucles founded Naxos, the earliest of the Greek colonies in Sicily.

8 A stretch of polygonal masonry forming part of the archaic city wall of Naxos, which associated finds suggest should be dated before the last quarter of the sixth century B.C. Compare the walls of later date in plates 27, 46, 47, 58 and 59. See G. V. Gentili, *Fasti Archaeologici*, IX, 1956 (relating to 1954), no. 2163, where fig. 36 shows the wall in process of excavation.

9 Segesta: the unfinished Doric temple (late fifth century B.C.) viewed from the acropolis (Monte Várvaro). The peristyle and entablature were erected though not completed in detail: little progress was made with the construction of the interior before the work was abandoned. See also plate 65.

10 Segesta: the auditorium and part of the stage buildings of the Hellenistic theatre, which is built into the side of Monte Várvaro and commands a wide view of the Golfo di Castellamare seen here in the background. The site of Segesta, amid majestic scenery and still comparatively isolated, is one of the most tranquil and beautiful in all Sicily.

11 Selinus: an archaic metope now in the Museo Nazionale, Palermo, on which Europa in shown riding on the bull (Zeus in disguise) which transported her across the sea from Phoenicia to Crete. The sea is represented by the dolphins visible below the bull. This metope was discovered re-used in later defence works, and probably belonged to a shrine demolished to make way for one of the larger, later structures. It dates to the second quarter of the sixth century B.C., and measures 84 x 59 cm.

12 Selinus: Temple C, with part of the north peristyle and entablature replaced. This temple, of the second half of the sixth century B.C., stands

on the main acropolis of the city (see plan on page 49), and measures 23.9 x 63.8 m. on the stylobate, with 6 x 17 columns in the peristyle. In the foreground are the ruins of Temple D.

13 Selinus: Temple C, with a view to the east towards the Marinella plateau, where Temple E, now largely restored, is clearly distinguishable, with Temple F immediately to the left and, just visible between two columns of Temple C, the massive remains of Temple G, with part of one column still erect. The distant mountains emphasise the amount of cultivable land commanded by Selinus; the flatness of the nearer land-scape illustrates the city's lack of natural defences.

14 Gela: Silen antefix found in the Via Apollo, and dating *c.* 460 B.C. These antefixes are from 22 to 24 cm. high, and, while silens are especially in evidence, gorgons, birds and banqueters are also represented. For the silen type compare plate 61 (*b*) and the silen head of the famous tetra-drachma of Aetna, also by the 'Aetna Master'. See P. Orlandini, *Not. Scav*. (Ser. VIII), X, 1956, 229–36.

15 Gela: Pithos of Geloan workmanship found at Butera, 55 cm. high and with a diameter at the mouth of 41 cm. Its reddish clay is covered with a slip and decorated in white paint with a weeping-willow pattern; the handle on the right is restored. Now in the Museo Archeologico at Gela, this vase usefully illustrates the local trade which developed in the archaic period between Gela and the native settlements of the hinterland. See D. Adamesteanu, *Monumenti Antichi*, XLIV, 1958, 520, no. 7, with fig. 196.

16 Gela: Stamnos of the late seventh century B.C., now in the Museo Archeologico. It stands 13.5 cm. high and is 18 cm. across. The same pattern of decoration is repeated on the other side of the vase, save that two heraldically-facing griffins replace the more naturalistic birds here illustrated. The artistic style reflects the Rhodian origin of many of the settlers of Gela. See D. Adamesteanu, *Not. Scav.* (Ser. VIII), X, 1956, 317–18.

17 Acragas: The 'Temple of Concord', so named by mistaken association with a Latin inscription found nearby; the correct dedication is not

known. Built about 460 B.C., it measures 16.9 x 39.4 m. on the stylobate, and has 6 x 13 columns in the peristyle. Restored not injudiciously in the eighteenth century, it is one of the best surviving examples of Doric temple-architecture of the classical period, and the warm texture of the local stone makes it particularly attractive at sunrise and sunset.

18 Acragas: The temple of Zeus Olympius, showing the buttressed curtain wall of the north side of the *cella* in the foreground (see plan on page 79). The unfinished building, of which the architectural details are uncertain, measured 52.9 x 110 m. In the background are visible the late sixth-century 'Temple of Hercules' and in the further distance the 'Temple of Concord' (see plate 17). The temples are strung out along the ridge bounding the city on the seaward side, and are now connected, conveniently for the sightseer, by a special road.

19 The coast at Heraclea Minoa. Such scenery as this emphasises the agricultural riches which Sicily offered to the Greek settlers and the wildness of the terrain they set themselves to conquer. For the modern traveller it suggests the strange mixture of warmth and desolation which is one of Sicily's principal attractions.

20 Locri: The fifth-century Ionic temple in the district near the sea known as Marasà. It measures 17.4 x 43.8 m. on the stylobate, and had a peristyle of 6 x 17 columns. The site was fully cleared during the past decade, and the Ionic base restored and re-erected. The author's wife is seated on the east wall of the temple, and beyond it may be seen the large altar which lay parallel with it.

21 Locri: The Ionic temple replaced a much smaller shrine of the archaic period, which itself went through two phases after originating as a sanctuary in the seventh century B.C. The small temple here shown had its axis at a slight angle to that of its larger successor, and was apparently a plain and unpretentious building with a small porch at the east end.

22 Locri: A restored terracotta group of a horseman, probably one of the Dioscuri, supported by a sphinx. Now in the Museo Nazionale at Reggio di Calabria, the complete figure stands some 140 cm. high, and

is to be dated to the mid-fifth century B.C. It apparently served as an *akroterion* for the Doric temple in the district known as Marafioti. See P. Orsi, *Not. Scav.* (Ser. V), VIII, 1911, Supplemento 40–9.

23 Posidonia (Paestum): The west end of the 'Temple of Ceres' as drawn by Thomas Major and published in his volume *The Ruins of Paestum otherwise Posidonia in Magna Graecia* (London, 1768). The artist has taken liberties with the topography by inserting the 'Temple of Neptune' close by to the left, but has given a more faithful rendering of the architectural details.

24 Posidonia (Paestum): The north and east sides of the 'Basilica'. Built about 530 B.C., this temple, which was dedicated to Hera, measured 24.5 x 54.3 m. on the stylobate, and had an unusual number of columns in the peristyle (9 x 18), with three columns *in antis* in the porch and a single row of eight columns, of equal size with those of the peristyle, down the centre of the *cella*. A loop cut in the stone to facilitate lifting by ropes may be seen in the end surviving block of the epistyle above the columns of the north colonnade.

25 Metapontum: The 'Tavole Paladine'. To be dated to the end of the sixth century B.C., this temple was much smaller than the Paestan basilica, with 6 x 12 columns in the peristyle and measuring about 15.8 x 33.2 m. on the stylobate. Its internal arrangements are uncertain. The flat, spreading echinus characteristic of the archaic period is noticeable here as in the preceding Paestan examples. See also plate 63.

26 Elea (Velia): The substructures of the fifth-century temple underlying the medieval castle at the seaward end of the acropolis. It has been suggested that it was dedicated to Athena. The masonry is careful and sophisticated work, illustrative of Elean prosperity at that period and of the ability of western artisans to rival the craftsmanship of Aegean Greece.

27 Elea (Velia): A retaining wall of the fifth century beside the agora, supporting a road at a higher level. The position of the agora in the curve of the hills demanded careful landscaping; the quality of the masonry provides its own commentary on the technique of the builders.

28 Elea (Velia): The sanctuary of Poseidon Asphaleios from the east. A saddle invisible in the photograph separates this part of the acropolis from the promontory with the watch-tower and fifth-century temple. This precinct was open to the sky, flanked by walls on three sides, and it was found to contain a number of altars and bases for dedicatory *stelae*. The *stele* in the foreground, here seen from the back, is illustrated in plate 53.

29 Gallic coins in imitation of the gold stater (didrachma) of Philip II of Macedon (359–336). B.C. That on the left recognisably reproduces a version of the laureate Apollo-head and the two-horse chariot, with the legend ΦΙΛΙΠΠΟΥ, of its original. That on the right has converted the designs into curvilinear and more abstract forms of a type with which the Celtic artist felt himself more at home.

30 Massalia (Marseilles): The Greek theatre at the time of its excavation (1946). The site, near the Vieux Port, which was cleared in consequence of war damage, has now been reclaimed for the business purposes of the modern city. This photograph witnesses the historic moment when the Greek character of the theatre seats at last confirmed a physical link between Marseilles and the architecture of its Greek past.

31 The 'Krater of Vix', a bronze volute-krater discovered in a Celtic burial of Hallstatt IIb type at Vix (Côte d'Or) and now in the museum of Châtillon-sur-Seine, some four miles away. It stands 1.64 m. high and is apparently of Tarentine or Laconian origin, to be dated *c.* 520 B.C. The figure frieze is 14 cm. in height, and shows a procession of warriors alternately on foot or in a four-horse chariot.

32 and 33 The 'Krater of Vix': Two details of the frieze, illustrating the quality of craftsmanship and design exemplified in every particular. The figures were fitted separately to the body of the vase, each figure having a letter scratched on its back to correspond with a similar letter marked on the vase at the point where it was to be attached. The letters are characteristically Laconian.

34 Himera: The north peristyle and *cella*-wall of the temple of Nike (Victory) built to commemorate the victory of Gelon over the Carthaginians

in 480 B.C. and demolished by the latter seventy-one years later. It was a regular Doric temple, measuring some 22.5 x 56 m. on the stylobate and with a peristyle of 6 x 14 columns. A lion's head which formed part of its cornice is illustrated in plate 67.

35 Pompeii: The Greek temple in the 'Foro Triangolare', the oldest part of the city. It was much altered in later times, but apparently had seven columns on the short sides of the peristyle and eleven on the flanks. The stylobate is unusually broad in relation to its length (17.25 x 17.8 m.). Built *c.* 550 B.C., it had been dismantled long before the eruption of A.D. 79.

36 Mount Erice (Eryx) near Trapani. This precipitous and almost impregnable stronghold was held against the Romans for three years (244–241 B.C.) by the Carthaginian Hamilcar Barca, who was himself besieging a Roman garrison in the sanctuary of Venus Erycina at the topmost point. The remains of the temple underlie the medieval castle. Erice dominated the 'Carthaginian corner' of Sicily, and the present town, which preserves its medieval character in its narrow, quiet streets, has a particular charm.

37 The inscribed base for a tripod (long since vanished) dedicated at Delphi by Gelon, tyrant of Syracuse (*c.* 490–*c.* 478), and standing near the temple of Apollo. The inscription reads 'Gelon, the son of Deinomenes, of Syracuse made this dedication to Apollo: Bion, the son of Diodorus, of Miletus made the tripod and the image of Victory.'

38 Bronze helmet dedicated at Olympia by Hieron, tyrant of Syracuse (*c.* 478–*c.* 466), after his defeat of the Etruscans in a naval battle off Cumae in 474 B.C. It is now in the British Museum. The inscription reads 'Hiaron, the son of Deinomenes, and the Syracusans—Tyrrhenian spoils from Cumae for Zeus.'

39 Syracuse: The temple of Athena. The view from within the present cathedral shows the north peristyle of the fifth-century temple (*c.* 470 B.C.), which measured about 22 x 55 m. on the stylobate and was a regular Doric building with a peristyle of 6 x 14 columns. The peristyle was

walled up and openings cut in the walls of the *cella* to convert the temple into a Christian church with a nave and two aisles.

40 Syracuse: The theatre. William Wilkins published this view in his survey *The Antiquities of Magna Graecia*, of 1807. The aqueduct and nymphaeum then served the purposes of a mill and market garden, and animals grazed amid the theatre seats.

41 Syracuse: The theatre after excavation, and viewed in the opposite direction. The mill-house still survives as a landmark. The town of Syracuse and the Great Harbour may be seen in the distance: nearer at hand is the 200-metre length of the altar of Hieron II. The theatre as it now appears is that of Hieron, with Roman alterations. The trapezoidal plan of the earliest theatre is, however, discernible in the cutting at the foot of the seats.

42 Syracuse: Two coins, both ten-drachma pieces, commemorating two great Syracusan victories. (*a*) is the *Demareteion* of 480–479 B.C., showing a head of Arethusa surrounded by dolphins and, on the reverse, a two-horse chariot, with in the exergue a Punic lion trampled under foot. (*b*) is a more modern version, by the designer Cimon, of the same theme, commemorating the defeat of the Athenians in 413 B.C. On the reverse, the charioteer of a four-horse chariot is crowned by a flying Victory, while captured Athenian arms are shown in the exergue.

43 Syracuse: The fort Euryalus. The complicated entrance-gate to the city on the northern side of the spur on which the fort stands, and overlooked by the main defences. The bay of Augusta and the peninsula of Magnisi (Thapsos) are visible in the background. The double gate was enfiladed by converging walls, and anyone entering was forced into a zigzag route which gave the defenders the maximum opportunity to deal with him.

44 Syracuse: Euryalus. The mounts for the heavy artillery which formed an important element in Archimedes' defensive scheme. In front of this massive emplacement were impressive and complicated outworks as well as three deep entrenchments, of which the innermost may be seen in the foreground. See A. W. Lawrence, *Journal of Hellenic Studies*, LXVI, 1946, 102–3.

45 Detail of the treaty between Athens and Dionysius I of Syracuse, 367 B.C. The stone, a marble *stele*, was found in 1837 on the Athenian acropolis and is now in the Epigraphical Museum at Athens (I.G., II², 105+523). This section comprises lines 9 to 28 of the 44-line document and contains the conditions of mutual support in time of war which formed the kernel of the agreement. Besides its historical value, this inscription is a useful illustration of the epigraphical style of the second quarter of the fourth century B.C.

46 Gela: The city walls on Capo Soprano, which formed part of the defences when Gela was revived and rebuilt by Timoleon. The efficacy of this section was progressively reduced by the movement of the sand-dunes which eventually engulfed and preserved it, and new upper courses in mud-brick were added at least twice. A perspex canopy has now been erected to protect its remarkable state of preservation.

47 Tyndaris: The city walls. Elements of the defences of Tyndaris go back to its foundation by Dionysius I; other sections belong to the period of the Roman colony. But the greater part of the surviving walls formed part of the city's revival under Timoleon, and offer a striking example of the masonry of the period.

48 Tyndaris, viewed from the east. The strength and suitability of the site chosen by Dionysius for his colony show to advantage at a distance: the promontory is joined to the mainland by a low saddle, and at other points is well protected by precipitous cliffs. These latter carried their own dangers, and the prosperity of the city did not really recover after a section of it slid into the sea in the Roman period.

49 Acrae (Palazzolo Acreide): The small bouleuterion or council-house beside the theatre, large enough only for three rows of seats and a podium for the president and speaker. It seems to belong to the period of building activity attested for this small city under the beneficent rule of Hieron II.

50 Morgantina (Serra Orlando): A view of the agora and the acropolis, looking towards the east. Catania lies beyond the distant hills, and the outline of Mt Etna is just visible. The agora lay on two levels divided by

a monumental stairway and between two slopes: on the eastern slope a stoa was backed by a series of residential terraces.

51 Morgantina: The monumental stairway of the agora. Since this photograph was taken (spring 1961), the slope on the west side has been excavated to reveal a theatre. The systematisation of the agora was apparently begun in the period of Timoleon and Agathocles, and the city declined after the Roman conquest.

52 Posidonia (Paestum): An inscription of the Roman Republican period, when the formerly Greek and later Lucanian city had been refounded as a Latin colony in 273 B.C. and absorbed into the Roman organisation of Italy. A list of names, perhaps of city-officials, is recorded on the stone, five of them being visible on the face illustrated.

53 Elea (Velia): The sandstone *stele* (see plate 28) which still stands to mark the sanctuary of Poseidon Asphaleios. The character of the lettering suggests that it was erected in the fourth century B.C.

54 Elea (Velia). By the time of this inscription, which dates approximately to the beginning of the Christian era, Velia had become Romanised, and the honours accorded to Caius Iulius Naso are expressed in Latin as well as in Greek. The round base (S.E.G., XVIII, 417) stands at present beside the medieval watch-tower on the acropolis.

55 (*a*): An example of the silver coinage of Hieron II of Syracuse, bearing the ruler's own portrait. Other coins of the series show the heads of his queen Philistis and his son Gelon (who predeceased him).
(*b*) and (*c*): Obverse and reverse of a silver *denarius* of Sextus Pompeius, 39–36 B.C., showing the lighthouse at Messana, with a warship beside it, and the figure of the monster Scylla with a double tail. The legend reads MAG[NVS] PIVS IMP[ERATOR] ITER[VM] and PRAEF[ECTVS] CLAS[SI] ET ORAE MARIT[IMAE] EX S[ENATVS] C[ONSVLTO].

56 Tyndaris: The theatre, in the form in which it was remodelled in the Roman period, when the lowest rows of seats were removed and the orchestra was adapted for wild-beast and gladiatorial shows. The original

version was built *c.* 100 B.C., and the remains of the stage-building are of that date. For a reconstruction see M. Bieber, *The History of the Greek and Roman Theater* (ed. 2, 1961), 170, fig. 602.

57 Posidonia (Paestum): An aerial view of the city centre, with north at the top of the photograph. The southern section of the city wall appears near the foot of the picture, with the three great temples and the area of the forum clearly distinguishable. The foundations of altars, shrines and other public and private buildings show more clearly than to the visitor on the ground the richness and complexity of the site.

58 Elea (Velia): A corner of the defence wall, with a road beside it, which runs from the acropolis inland along the ridge and links the sanctuaries strung along it much as at Acragas. Of fifth-century date, it will have played a vital part in the successful defence of the city against Lucanian pressure.

59 Tyndaris: A view inland from the highest part of the promontory near the theatre, showing the careful and elaborate defences on the landward side, the city's one weak point, built in the period of Timoleon. The land falls away sharply below the wall. See plates 47 and 48.

60 Megara Hyblaea: The torso of a *kouros* found in 1940 and now in the Museo Nazionale at Syracuse. It stands 1.19 m. high, and is of marble imported from the Aegean. On the right leg is an inscription which reads 'Of Somrotidas the physician, son of Mandrocles.' Style of sculpture and of inscription may be combined to date the figure *c.* 550–540 B.C. See G. M. A. Richter, *Kouroi* (ed. 2, 1960), 112, no. 134, with figs. 388–90.

61 (*a*): Tetradrachma of Gela, of the mid-fifth century B.C., showing the standard 'type' of the city—a man-headed bull representing the river Gelas.
(*b*): Tetradrachma of Naxos, of the same period, the work of the 'Aetna Master', showing on the reverse a silen with a kantharos of wine. The carefully sculptured treatment of the anatomy is especially remarkable.

62 Foce del Sele: A metope from the Temple of Hera, of the end of the sixth century B.C., the most complete of a series depicting girls who advance in pairs in processional dance in honour of the goddess, their attitudes skilfully varied. A chorus-leader occupies a metope to herself. The relief technique is lively and charming, and bears comparison with contemporary work in Aegean Greece.

63 Posidonia (Paestum): Two capitals of the 'Basilica', illustrating the archaic form of the echinus and the ring of sculptured leaves which decorated the transition between column-shaft and capital. This form of ornamentation is a peculiarity of Paestan Doric.

64 Posidonia (Paestum): The 'Temple of Neptune', from the south-west. Built at about the same time as the 'Temple of Concord' at Acragas, and like it one of the best preserved of Greek temples, it measures some 24.3 x 60 m. on the stylobate and has a peristyle of 6 x 14 columns. The columns of the *cella*, in two rows with a smaller row of columns superposed, survive to give unusually full evidence of the internal arrangements.

65 Segesta: A view of the unfinished Doric temple. See plate 9. Although the peristyle was completed as far as the entablature, the columns remained unfluted and the more elaborated details would have awaited the completion of the *cella* and the removal of the heavy building-tackle.

66 A Siculo-Ionic capital of Hellenistic date from Centuripae, now in the Museo Nazionale at Syracuse.

67 Himera: A lion's-head spout from the cornice of the Temple of Nike, now in the Museo Nazionale at Palermo. See plate 34.

68 Apulian stand for a *thymiaterion* (incense-burner), of the later fourth century, now in the Lewis Collection, Corpus Christi College, Cambridge, 32.6 cm. high, it shows a female head and an eros. See A. Cambitoglou, *Journal of Hellenic Studies*, LXXIV, 1954, 117, with plate VI, d.

69 Skyphos of the Apulian school, now in the same collection. It is 19.3 cm. high, and belongs to the ornate style of the mid-fourth century B.C., with much white and gold paint applied to the basic red and black of the vase. That this decoration is sometimes crudely added is illustrated by the Nike of this piece.

70 Bell-krater of Paestan style, signed by Python, now in the British Museum (F 149); it stands 56 cm. high. Alcmena appeals to Zeus for help against Antenor (left) and Amphitryon (right), and the god responds by sending rain, provided by the Hyades, to quench the flames of the altar to which the irate heroes are setting fire. See A. D. Trendall, *Paestan Pottery*, 56–7, with plate XV.

71 Caeretan hydria, from Cerveteri (Caere), now in the British Museum (B 59); J. M. Hemelrijk, *De Caeretaanse Hydriae*, no. 1. This vase, 43.5 cm. high, is the work of the Knee-painter and perhaps the earliest of the Caeretan group. Four warriors are shown in combat on either side of the vase, above a wide band of palmettes and lotus.

72 Fourth-century terracotta altar from Centuripae, now in the Museo Nazionale at Syracuse, depicting a lion attacking a bull. *Arulae* of various sizes and decorated with a variety of scenes are frequently met with in votive deposits in Sicily and Magna Graecia. See E. D. Van Buren, *Memoirs of the American Academy in Rome*, II, 1918, 15–53, and for a group recently discovered at Gela, P. Orlandini, *Mitteilungen des Deutschen Archaeologischen Instituts* (*Roemische Abteilung*), LXVI, 1958, 97–103.

73 Krater of Centuripae ware, with cover, now in the Museo Nazionale at Syracuse. Some 66 cm. high, it has plastic decoration in the form of lions' heads and a leaf and dart moulding below the lip, and has a painted scene of seated women and erotes. The background is pink, with flesh colour for the exposed parts of the body and grey and buff for clothes. This vase is illustrated in colour in L. Bernabò Brea, *Musei e Monumenti di Sicilia*, 1958, 59.

74 Bronze statuette of the fifth century B.C., found at Rhegium and now in the Museo Nazionale there. The *kore*, who is about 13 cm. high, wears a peplos with a decorated border and adjusts her hair with her right hand.

75 Miniature lion, some 5 cm. in length and here much enlarged, which probably formed part of the decoration of a bronze vessel such as the hydria of plate 76. It appears to have been found in Rhegium, and is now in the Museo Nazionale there.

76 Bronze hydria, found on the road between Gela and Licata, and now in the Museo Nazionale at Syracuse. Less ornate and less well-preserved than the examples found in the sanctuary of the Nymph at Posidonia, it has impressively flowing lines, and the handle ends in a well-executed decorative palmette.

77 Terracotta cornice of lion's-head spouts connected by a running frieze of lotus and palmettes, part of the Doric (Marafioti) temple at Locri, and now in the Museo Nazionale at Reggio di Calabria.

78 Terracotta gorgon, partly restored, now in the Museo Nazionale at Syracuse and probably a lateral *akroterion* of the archaic temple of Athena on Ortygia. Dating to the mid-sixth century B.C., the relief measures 56 x 50 cm., and is brilliantly coloured. See E. D. Van Buren, *Archaic Fictile Revetments in Sicily and Magna Graecia*, 158–9, no. 10.

79 Dedicatory *pinax* (terracotta plaque) from the sanctuary of Persephone at Locri, now in the Museo Nazionale at Reggio. This is the most complete of the long series, which is to receive its full publication by Dr Paola Zancani-Montuoro, and it shows Persephone and Pluto enthroned and holding offerings associated with their cult.

80 Silver decadrachma of Syracuse, by Evaenetus (late fifth century B.C.), with a particularly beautiful rendering of the head of the nymph Arethusa, the symbol and protectress of the city.

81 The Fountain of Arethusa at Syracuse, where a spring of fresh water still emerges close to the shore of the Great Harbour. The papyrus reeds grow wild here and at the Fonte Ciane, on the other side of the harbour beyond the Olympieum, and these are said to be the only places in Europe where they do so.

Index